lonely planet

Diving & Snorkeling

Chuuk Lagoon,
Pohnpei & Kosrae

Tim Rock

LONELY PLANET PUBLICATIONS
Melbourne • Oakland • London • Paris

Diving & Snorkeling Chuuk Lagoon, Pohnpei & Kosrae
- A Lonely Planet Pisces Book

1st edition
May, 2000

Published by
Lonely Planet Publications
192 Burwood Road, Hawthorn, Victoria 3122, Australia

Other offices
150 Linden Street, Oakland, California 94607, USA
10A Spring Place, London NW5 3BH, UK
1 rue du Dahomey, 75011 Paris, France

Photographs
All photographs by Tim Rock unless otherwise noted

Front cover photograph
Coral encrusted remnants of the Emily Flying Boat in
Chuuk Lagoon, by Tim Rock

Back cover photographs, by Tim Rock
Tubastrea corals come out at night to feed
A skull from a WWII victim rests on the seafloor
Sunset from Weno, Chuuk Lagoon

The images in this guide are available for licensing
from **Lonely Planet Images**
email: lpi@lonelyplanet.com.au

ISBN 1 86450 029 8

text & maps © Lonely Planet 2000
photographs © photographers as indicated 2000
illustrations by K & S Enterprises
dive site maps are Transverse Mercator projection

LONELY PLANET and the Lonely Planet logo are
trademarks of Lonely Planet Publications Pty Ltd.

Printed by H&Y Printing Ltd., Hong Kong

Contents

Diving Health & Safety 44

Diving in Chuuk Lagoon, Pohnpei & Kosrae 47

Chuuk Lagoon Dive Sites 52

Chuuk Lagoon Shipwrecks 54

Author

Tim Rock

Tim Rock attended the journalism program at the University of Nebraska, Omaha. He has been a professional broadcast and print photojournalist for 25 years, the majority of which have been spent in the Western and Indo Pacific reporting on environmental and conservation issues. His television series *Aquaquest Micronesia* was an Ace Award finalist. He has also produced six documentaries on the history and undersea fauna of the region. He has won the prestigious Excellence in the Use of Photography from the Society of Publisher's in Asia. He is the author of four other Lonely Planet Pisces diving and snorkeling guides to Palau, Bali, Guam & Yap and Papua New Guinea. Tim lives on Guam with his wife, Larie.

STEFANIE BRENDL

From the Author

For nearly two decades I have made regular visits to the Chuuk Lagoon to photograph and document the changing conditions of the wrecks and report new finds. Chuuk's sage of diving, Kimiuo Aisek, has been a dive buddy, a resource and a friend through this period, unselfishly sharing his wit, knowledge and time. I am grateful and feel fortunate to have such a true gentleman as a companion. I must also give honor to his son Gradvin, who has taken such giant strides in his father's footsteps.

On Pohnpei, I have shared many dives, treks and laughs with guide par excellence and divemaster Wendolin "Sweeper" Lionas. His great spirit, and the special generosity of Maryalice and Emensio Eperium, have made all of my visits exceptional.

On Kosrae, the warm and gracious hospitality of my friends Madison Nena, Geoff Raaschou, Katrina Adams and Bruce Brandt have made me see the superb potential and propriety of eco-tourism. To these fine folks and all others I have encountered in the FSM, I humbly give thanks.

Photography Notes

Tim Rock's photographic equipment includes Nikonos II, III, IV & V cameras, housed Nikons in Aquatica housings and Nikonos RSAF cameras and lenses. His strobes are made by Nikon and Ikelite. Land cameras are the F5, F100, Coolpix 950 and N90 by Nikon, with Nikkor lenses.

From the Publisher

This first edition was produced in Lonely Planet's U.S. office under direction from Roslyn Bullas, Pisces Books publishing manager. Senior Editor Debra Miller edited the text and selected photos. Emily Douglas designed the book and cover with her usual style and positive buoyancy. Sarah Hawkins Hubbard and Rachel Bernstein donned their proofreading masks and added valuable editing assistance. Cartographer Patrick Bock dived deep into the archives and historical accounts to create the maps, with help from Sara Nelson and U.S. cartography manager Alex Guilbert. Shelley Firth, Justin Marler and Hayden Foell plunged in with illustrative prowess. Portions of the text were adapted from Lonely Planet's *South Pacific* and *Micronesia*. Lindsay Brown reviewed the marine life section for scientific accuracy. Special thanks to Klaus Lindemann, whose *Hailstorm Over Truk Lagoon* helped us understand the story and scope of the battles that left so much wreckage in Chuuk Lagoon.

Lonely Planet Pisces Books

Lonely Planet acquired the Pisces line of diving and snorkeling books in 1997. The series is being developed and substantially revamped over the next few years. We welcome your comments and suggestions.

Pisces Pre-Dive Safety Guidelines

Before embarking on a scuba diving, skin diving or snorkeling trip, carefully consider the following to help ensure a safe and enjoyable experience:

- Possess a current diving certification card from a recognized scuba diving instructional agency (if scuba diving)
- Be sure you are healthy and feel comfortable diving
- Obtain reliable information about physical and environmental conditions at the dive site (e.g., from a reputable local dive operation)
- Be aware of local laws, regulations and etiquette about marine life and environment
- Dive at sites within your experience level; if possible, engage the services of a competent, professionally trained dive instructor or divemaster

Underwater conditions vary significantly from one region, or even site, to another. Seasonal changes can significantly alter site and dive conditions. These differences influence the way divers dress for a dive and what diving techniques they use.

There are special requirements for diving in any area, regardless of location. Before your dive, ask about environmental characteristics that can affect your diving and how trained local divers deal with these considerations.

Warning & Request

Things change—dive site conditions, regulations, topside information. Nothing stays the same for long. Your feedback on this book will be used to help update and improve the next edition. Excerpts from your correspondence may appear in *Planet Talk*, our quarterly newsletter, or *Comet*, our monthly email newsletter. Please let us know if you do not want your letter published or your name acknowledged.

Correspondence can be addressed to:
Lonely Planet Publications
Pisces Books
150 Linden Street
Oakland, CA 94607
email: pisces@lonelyplanet.com

Introduction

Chuuk, Pohnpei and Kosrae are just dots on the map in the vast Pacific Ocean, but each remote island jewel has a unique cultural character borne out of geographic remoteness, time-honored traditions and an almost mystical respect for the natural environment. These island states are vast—mostly stretches of ocean with occasional atolls dotting the seascape. Their distinctive land topographies give way to pristine hard coral reefs, prolific channels and diverse marine life, giving divers and snorkelers almost limitless opportunities.

These islands existed independently for centuries before explorers stumbled upon them and claimed them for various European countries. The native islanders had unique lifestyles that appeared to be shrouded in superstition and mystery.

The vast canals and basalt stone structures of Pohnpei's ancient city of Nan Madol made it one of the most incredible engineering feats in the Pacific. A similarly advanced civilization also existed in Kosrae. In Chuuk, each inner-lagoon island fiercely guarded its resources, and a unique form of martial arts developed in this atmosphere of imminent battle.

JAPAN	150°E	165°E	180°	165°W

PACIFIC OCEAN

30°N

Midway Islands (US)

Tropic of Cancer

Northern Mariana Islands (US)

PHILIPPINES

Hawaii (US)

15°N

Guam (US)

Yap

FEDERATED STATES OF MICRONESIA

MARSHALL ISLANDS

Palau

CHUUK LAGOON

POHNPEI

KOSRAE

Equator

PAPUA NEW GUINEA

INDONESIA

SOLOMON ISLANDS

SAMOA

15°S

VANUATU

FIJI

AUSTRALIA

New Caledonia (Fr)

TONGA

After years of Japanese occupation between WWI and WWII, these islands were administered by the U.S. as Trust Territories. The U.S. was not a great overseer and only minimally developed the infrastructure. When the trust dissolved in the 1980s, Truk (now Chuuk), Ponape (now Pohnpei), and Kusaie (now Kosrae) joined Yap to become an independent nation known as the Federated States of Micronesia (FSM).

Despite this political umbrella, each state is unique. For instance, in Kosrae, the Congregational Church plays a vital role in everyday life, while in Chuuk clan relationships remain an important factor. Over the last 15 years Pohnpei has rapidly developed into the most westernized state, but traditional leadership continues to play an important role.

Old mines make an artificial breakwater at Param Island in Chuuk Lagoon.

Today, the main islands serve as both capitals and population centers and although independence brought periods of growth and development, the tourism industry is still quite new. In Chuuk, for example, only Weno has electricity, paved roads and cars. On Chuuk's other islands people still lead a subsistence lifestyle.

As you fly in to Chuuk Lagoon, you'll see that the broad outer reef of this immense raised atoll is fringed in palm-covered islands that have sandy beaches and little relief. Inside the lagoon, lush, higher islands poke up from the generally calm waters. From the air, it's hard to imagine that more than 60 artifact-laden WWII ships and planes—a significant portion of the Japanese fleet—rest on the seafloor. The array of ships—with varying depths, and historical and natural attractions—keeps Chuuk Lagoon at the forefront of wreck diving.

Pohnpei's outer barrier reef is vast and pocked with blue holes and meandering channels. As you fly into Kolonia, you see waterfalls gushing from the mountains. The cloud cover over the razorbacked peaks explains why Pohnpei is one of the rainiest places on Earth. The island's host of rivers feed a mangrove system that keeps the inner lagoon rich in nutrients. Add two eye-popping atolls—Ahnd and Pakein—and it's easy to understand Pohnpei's draw.

Kosrae remained pretty much off the snorkeled path until the early 1990s, when dive exploration started to happen. Signs of development on Kosrae are few, and the rugged ridges of the heavily jungled mounts dominate the shoreline. The barrier reef is a blend of aquas and greens; in places the reef plunges deeply just offshore. Kosrae's hard corals are among the healthiest in the Pacific. The variety and size of these reefs, located east of most typhoon disturbances, make them a biologist's delight.

This book describes dive sites on the main islands of Chuuk, Pohnpei and Kosrae, along with nearby atoll sites in Chuuk and Pohnpei. You will find detailed site information, including the kinds of marine life you can expect to see, depth range and recommended diver expertise. Many of the Chuuk wreck descriptions are accompanied by sketches and historical accounts of the ships' wartime demise.

General information on each island's history, topside practicalities, activities and attractions, and culture will help you enjoy your stay. Each island is charming in its own way. Any dive trip is enhanced by some exposure to local cultures and traditions—this is especially true on these wonderful Pacific outposts.

Pohnpeian children perform ancient chants and traditional dances at an island celebration.

Overview

Chuuk, Pohnpei and Kosrae are located in the north-western part of the central Pacific Ocean. They, along with Yap, compose the political entity known as the FSM. The states border one another—Kosrae is the easternmost, moving westward to Pohnpei, Chuuk and Yap. (For information on Yap, see Lonely Planet's *Diving & Snorkeling Guam & Yap.*) While these 607 islands—all part of the Caroline Islands—are sprinkled across more than a million sq miles (2.6 million sq km), the country's total land mass amounts to only 271 sq miles (702 sq km). Of the islands in this guide, Pohnpei has almost half the land mass, but more than 50% of the population lives in Chuuk (about 51,000 people), while about 35,000 live in Pohnpei and 7,500 in Kosrae.

The people of the FSM are classified as Micronesians, although some inhabitants of Pohnpei are Polynesian. They are actually a heterogeneous mixture with different customs and traditions, but bound together by recent history and common aspirations for independence.

Cultural similarities are evident by the importance each state places on traditional customs, family and clan systems. These are not wealthy islands and a subsistence economy is still very prominent in the outer islands and even in the state centers.

While traditional religions still exist on the islands, Christianity—including Catholicism, Baptist Protestant and Seventh-Day Adventist—now dominates.

An Eten Island girl carries laundry just washed in the sea.

Geography

Chuuk

Chuuk is one of the largest and most scenic atolls in the Pacific. Chuuk Lagoon has 15 large islands surrounded by a near-circular 140-mile (224km) barrier reef. Weno, Tol, Tonoas, Fefan and Uman are the most populated islands and Weno serves as the capital and commercial center. Five passages cut through the protective reef, allowing ships to enter the deep harbors.

The high islands in Chuuk's inner-lagoon are remnants of a submerged, long-dormant volcano cone, while the outer reef islands are remainders of the crater rim. The fringing reef islands have sandy beaches and are ideal for day picnics and decompression stops. The volcanic basalt rock and rich soil form an odd combination, but breadfruit thrives in this environment as do coconut palm, banana and mango trees.

Chuuk State has nearly 200 outlying lower islands, also mainly atolls with small islands surrounding an azure inner lagoon.

Chuuk Lagoon's outer barrier reef.

Coral Atolls

Charles Darwin was the first to recognize that atolls are made from coral growth that has built up around the edges of a submerged volcanic mountain peak.

In a scenario played out over hundreds of thousands of years, coral first builds up around the shores of a high island producing a fringing reef. Then, as the island begins to slowly sink under its own weight, the coral continues to grow upward at about the same rate. This forms a barrier reef that is separated from the shore by a lagoon. By the time the island has completely submerged, the coral growth has become a base for an atoll, circling the place where the mountain top used to be.

The classic atoll shape is roughly oval, with islands of coral rubble and sand built up on the higher points of the reef. There are usually breaks in the reef rim large enough for boats to enter the sheltered lagoon.

Pohnpei

Pohnpei State includes Pohnpei's main island (the largest in the FSM); eight atolls, 25 smaller islands within a barrier reef; and 137 widely scattered coral atolls, often referred to as outer islands. Pohnpei's total land mass equals 133 sq miles (343 sq km).

The main island is divided into six municipalities including Kolonia, which is the island's commercial center and the state capital. The FSM national government headquarters are 5km from Kolonia, in Palikir.

Most of Pohnpei's shoreline is covered by mangrove swamps, but nearby reef islands boast beautiful sand beaches. The island's most prominent feature is Sokehs Rock, a steep cliff face often compared to Hawaii's Diamond Head. The ancient stone city of Nan Madol is Micronesia's best-known archeological site.

Pohnpei's interior consists of rugged basalt mountains often shrouded in clouds, and lush, deep valleys. Nahna Laud (Big Mountain) and Ngihn Eni (Ghost Tooth) are the highest peaks, with heights exceeding 2,500ft (650m). With an annual average rainfall exceeding 400 inches (1,016cm) in the upper rain forest, Pohnpei gets plenty of rain, earning its reputation as one of the wettest places on the planet.

Kosrae

Kosrae is the easternmost of the Outer Caroline Islands and, oddly, has no atoll or outer islands anywhere in the state's waters. The main island is connected to Lelu Island by a causeway; together they comprise the FSM's smallest land mass at only 43 sq miles (112 sq km). The administration center and most of the commercial activities are concentrated in Lelu.

Kosrae is highlighted by a mountain range dubbed the "Sleeping Lady," which overlooks much of the main populated area and dominates the landscape. Its

Sleeping Lady

Looking south across Kosrae's Lelu Harbor toward Tofol you'll see the rugged profile of the "Sleeping Lady" mountain range. To view the profile, imagine a woman lying on her back facing southeast, with her hair flowing out behind her head. The pointy "breasts" are easy to spot.

Legend has it that the gods were angry with a woman so they laid her in the sea in a sleeping position and turned her into the island of Kosrae. That woman was then menstruating accounts for the rich red soil found in the jungle at the place between her "thighs." Kosraean men used to trek into the interior to gather the red soil from this sacred place and use it to make paint for their canoes.

highest point, Mt. Finkol, rises to some 2,060ft (628m). Over 70% of the island is deep valleys and high ridges. Thus, all villages are coastal.

Heavy rainfall feeds numerous perennial streams. The freshwater, with its load of minerals and sediments, inhibits coral growth in estuarine habitats where streams mix with salt water. Lelu, Okat and Utwe are the three deep natural harbors that attracted whalers in the 19th century. Okat and Utwe are adjoined by large tracts of mangrove swamp, which make up another 15% of the landmass.

History

Early History

Most linguistic and archaeological evidence indicates that the FSM islands were first discovered and settled between two and three thousand years ago. The first settlers are often described as Austronesian speakers, possessing horticultural skills and highly sophisticated maritime knowledge. These first settlers are thought to have migrated eastward from Southeast Asia to Yap. From there, some migrated south to Papua New Guinea, the Solomon Islands and New Caledonia, and later to Kiribati and the Marshall Islands.

Oral histories of the Micronesian people indicate close affiliations among other island societies comprising the present-day FSM. Medieval Pohnpei was ruled by the Saundeleurs, a tyrannical royal dynasty that reigned from Nan Madol, an elaborate canal city of stone fortresses and temples.

Pohnpei's Nan Madol was manually constructed out of huge, heavy basalt pillars.
These ruins at Nan Dowas are the most intact remnants of the ancient city.

By 1400, Kosrae was unified under one paramount chief, or *tokosra*, who ruled from the island of Lelu. It became the center of a complex feudal society that warred with Pohnpei and settled Chuuk in the 15th century. Commoners lived on the main island while the royalty and their retainers lived inside more than 100 basalt-walled compounds on Lelu and nearby islets. With its canal system and coral streets, the fortressed island would have rivaled its medieval counterparts in Europe.

Chuuk is believed to have been settled by people from Kosrae in the 1400s. Legend tells of Chief Sowukachaw, who came to Chuuk in an ocean-going canoe with his son. The chief was credited with bringing new breadfruit trees to the islands and developing a food preservation method, which was considered highly important. Breadfruit is still a staple today.

Europeans

The first Europeans arrived in the FSM around 1526. The Spanish, arriving later, claimed sovereignty over the Caroline Islands until 1899, when Spain sold its holdings to Germany.

Pohnpei's German bell tower is a reminder of European occupation.

Pohnpei's 1910 to 1911 Sokehs Rebellion was sparked when a Pohnpei man working on a labor gang on Sokehs Island was beaten by a German overseer. The Pohnpeians killed the overseer and instigated the unsuccessful revolt. The Germans took revenge by blockading Kolonia and sending Melanesian troops up Sokehs Ridge. Seventeen rebel leaders were executed and thrown into a mass grave.

In 1914, Japan took control of the islands and the population influx surpassed that of the locals. Chuuk's huge, sheltered lagoon became the Japanese Imperial Fleet's most important central Pacific forward base, so impenetrable that it was called the "Gibraltar of the Pacific." The Japanese developed with great vigor, creating prosperous times for Chuuk and the surrounding islands.

WWII brought an abrupt end to the relative prosperity. On February 17, 1944, the U.S. Navy air-bombed the Japanese fleet. The attacks took the Japanese by surprise—the air raids happened so suddenly that Chuuk's Japanese air defenses were disabled and its ships were summarily sunk. Some 50 ships went down in the melee and over 150 airplanes were disabled. Most of the crippled ships and planes lie on the seafloor today.

Diving History

Chuuk Lagoon
Diving first came to Chuuk in the mid-1960s, pioneered by Kimiuo Aisek. His quest for fish made him try a dive on one of the lagoon's sunken WWII Japanese ships. His discovery of the ships' beauty attracted *National Geographic* and ensuing media attention, making Chuuk Lagoon a world-renowned dive destination. In the early '80s, Aisek and historian Klaus Lindemann identified even more wrecks. Live-aboards came to the lagoon in the early '90s.

Historian Klaus Lindemann examines the engine room of a small wreck.

Pohnpei
Since the late 1970s, Village Hotel owners Patti and Bob Arthur have been leaders in eco-tourism by promoting environmental and cultural sensitivity in tourism. Through the resort, they pioneered Pohnpei diving by putting it on the dive-destination map. Further dive-site exploration followed in the '90s by Wendolin Lionas of Iet Ehu Tours and historical preservation officers Emensio Eperium and Edgar Santos. Together with ex-pat Hal Sheets they thoroughly explored Pohnpei's perimeter and two outer atolls.

Kosrae
Diving is new to Kosrae and its development is thanks to Bruce Brandt of Kosrae Village Resort and Jeff Raaschou of Kosrae Nautilus Resort. Both of these operators brought organized diving to the island in the '90s, training divemasters and even government conservation officers. Prior to that, local entrepreneurs would take divers out using old catamaran fishing boats that had been donated by the Japanese government for public use. There are now more than 50 buoyed sites around Kosrae and many new sites still beckon proper exploration.

Trust Territory

After the war, the UN established the Trust Territory of the Pacific Islands, which involved six districts: the Northern Marianas, Pohnpei (then including Kosrae), Chuuk, Yap, the Marshall Islands and Palau. The U.S. was given exclusive rights to administer the islands and to establish and maintain military bases while preventing other nations from doing the same.

Under UN guidelines, the U.S. was obliged to foster the development of political and economic institutions, with the ultimate goal of helping Micronesians achieve self-sufficiency. The U.S. had little experience in developing new nations so it adopted a relatively hands-off approach, letting the islanders go on as before, while administering them governmentally. This, in hindsight, was a poor choice, evident by today's extreme government dependency.

In the 1960s the U.S. began yielding to Micronesian aspirations toward self-government. The establishment of the Peace Corps brought teachers to Micronesia, but the young teachers also brought '60s notions of drugs, sex and political reform to the islands. While the drugs and sex clashed with the local cultures, the politics thrived.

The former Japanese hospital on Tonoas is now a tourist attraction.

Becoming States

The U.S. had initially expected that the Trust Territories would become one Micronesian nation, but this was not to be. In 1965 the U.S. agreed to the formation of the Congress of Micronesia, a two-house legislature made up of elected representatives from all island groups to discuss their future political status.

In January 1978 the people of the Northern Marianas, based in Saipan, opted to become U.S. citizens under U.S. Commonwealth status. Later that year the other Trust Territory districts voted on a common constitution, which, among other things, would allow nuclear submarines to enter their waters and nuclear armaments to be stored on land. Devastating 1950s atomic bomb tests at Bikini Island and other Marshall outposts prompted both Marshall Islanders and Palauans to vote against the referendum. Yap, Chuuk, Pohnpei and Kosrae voted in favor, becoming the FSM.

Laundry hangs to dry in the former Japanese headquarters on Eten.

Compact of Free Association

In October 1982 the FSM signed a 15-year Compact of Free Association with the U.S., which was officially implemented in November 1986. The economic trade-off was good for this emerging nation. The compact guaranteed funding from the U.S., the use of the U.S. dollar and postal system, and military protection that would negate the need for these nations to establish costly military forces.

In theory the compact allows the new states to manage their internal affairs, although their relationships with other nations are at times governed by U.S. diplomatic relations. The FSM islands, with the exception of Yap, have resident CAT units (Civic Action Teams) that provide major engineering assistance to the governments, maintaining roads and erecting civic buildings and basketball courts. In all, it has been an amicable relationship but no economic boon for the FSM. Economic development is left to each state government, the national government and to private entrepreneurs. It is hoped, once the compact dissolves, that the FSM's relationship with the U.S. will be maintained, although the extent of financial, infrastructural and military assistance is, as yet, unknown.

WWII Shipwrecks, the History

By far, Chuuk's main attraction is its sunken WWII Japanese fleet. The lagoon, with 140 miles (225km) of outer barrier reef, 11 high islands and five passages, was considered an ideal, naturally protected harbor in the middle of Micronesia. This same protection, however, also made it a difficult place to escape—an irony that caused the Japanese fleet's demise.

The U.S. taking of Chuuk was a strategic necessity. The U.S. and Allied forces had been pushing through the western and southern Pacific in 1943 and early 1944. The plan was to create a pincer movement by pushing upward from Papua New Guinea and then east-to-west from Chuuk, culminating in the taking of Guam, the Marianas and the Philippines. The U.S. perceived Chuuk as the perfect staging area from which to move into Japan and defeat the enemy. Americans simply had to fly in, destroy Chuuk's shipping resources, and then pass it by.

In the days prior to the attack, destroyers, subs, cruisers and nine aircraft carriers of the U.S. Task Force 58 maneuvered into position. They planned to neutralize the Japanese aircraft first, destroy supply facilities, and then strike the helpless ships.

It was still dark the morning of February 17, 1944, when the Japanese detected the large group of planes approaching. An alert sounded at sunrise. The Japanese were shocked when a hundred American planes descended like massive flies on the lagoon. This attack was relentlessly followed by nine more waves, totaling 450 planes. Japanese intelligence failed and the fleet was completely overwhelmed by the onslaught of so many carrier-based planes. Seventy-seven Japanese planes scrambled to defend Chuuk, but 37 were lost before ever engaging in battle.

Airplane fuselage sitting partially underwater off Weno.

U.S. Dauntlesses, Hellcats and Avenger torpedo bombers filled the skies and emptied their loads. The results were devastating. Japanese attempts to find the carrier fleet and attack it were virtually useless. Runways and planes were destroyed on Eten, the main air base.

The raids continued against near-futile Japanese retaliation. The U.S. staged another pre-dawn raid on February 18th, and the attacks continued. No Japanese planes could counter because they were either damaged or unable to take off—the runways were filled with craters.

In two days, Chuuk was shaken and broken. Over four hundred planes were rendered useless; more than 50 ships were sunk or sinking; support and communications facilities were destroyed or in flames, and thousands of Japanese troops were left behind without food, support and ammunition. Casualties on land alone numbered around 600. American casualties numbered less than 30, as the U.S. submarine Tang rescued 28 drowning airmen. Only 22 U.S. aircraft were lost.

For months, local people lived in fear, as did the surviving Japanese soldiers and sailors. There were more raids on Chuuk. In April, the Japanese long-range submarine I-169 was sunk during a high-level bombing raid. Many Chuukese people knew nothing of Americans but to fear them. Locals fished and gathered food at night, fearful an American plane would fly in at any moment and attack, mistaking them for the enemy Japanese. For almost two years the people of Chuuk struggled before the war was brought to its atomic end.

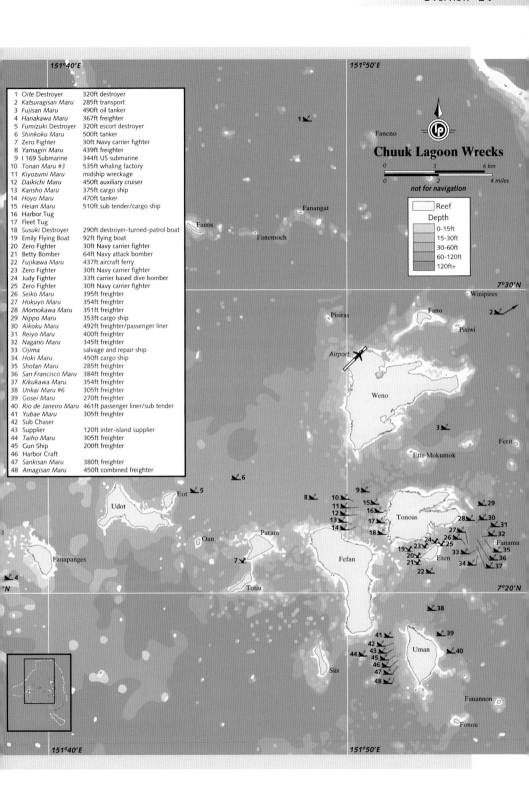

1	*Oite* Destroyer	320ft destroyer
2	*Katsuragisan Maru*	285ft transport
3	*Fujisan Maru*	490ft oil tanker
4	*Hanakawa Maru*	367ft freighter
5	*Fumizuki* Destroyer	320ft escort destroyer
6	*Shinkoku Maru*	500ft tanker
7	Zero Fighter	30ft Navy carrier fighter
8	*Yamagiri Maru*	439ft freighter
9	I 169 Submarine	344ft US submarine
10	*Tonan Maru #3*	535ft whaling factory
11	*Kiyozumi Maru*	midship wreckage
12	*Daikichi Maru*	450ft auxiliary cruiser
13	*Kansho Maru*	375ft cargo ship
14	*Hoyo Maru*	470ft tanker
15	*Heian Maru*	510ft sub tender/cargo ship
16	Harbor Tug	
17	Fleet Tug	
18	*Susuki* Destroyer	290ft destroyer-turned-patrol boat
19	Emily Flying Boat	92ft flying boat
20	Zero Fighter	30ft Navy carrier fighter
21	Betty Bomber	64ft Navy attack bomber
22	*Fujikawa Maru*	437ft aircraft ferry
23	Zero Fighter	30ft Navy carrier fighter
24	Judy Fighter	33ft carrier based dive bomber
25	Zero Fighter	30ft Navy carrier fighter
26	*Seiko Maru*	395ft freighter
27	*Hokuyo Maru*	354ft freighter
28	*Momokawa Maru*	351ft freighter
29	*Nippo Maru*	353ft cargo ship
30	*Aikoku Maru*	492ft freighter/passenger liner
31	*Reiyo Maru*	400ft freighter
32	*Nagano Maru*	345ft freighter
33	*Ojima*	salvage and repair ship
34	*Hoki Maru*	450ft cargo ship
35	*Shotan Maru*	285ft freighter
36	*San Francisco Maru*	384ft freighter
37	*Kikukawa Maru*	354ft freighter
38	*Unkai Maru #6*	305ft freighter
39	*Gosei Maru*	270ft freighter
40	*Rio de Janeiro Maru*	461ft passenger liner/sub tender
41	*Yubae Maru*	305ft freighter
42	Sub Chaser	
43	Supplier	120ft inter-island supplier
44	*Taiho Maru*	305ft freighter
45	Gun Ship	200ft freighter
46	Harbor Craft	
47	*Sankisan Maru*	380ft freighter
48	*Amagisan Maru*	450ft combined freighter

Chuuk Lagoon Wrecks

0   3   6 km
0   2   4 miles

not for navigation

Reef
Depth
0-15ft
15-30ft
30-60ft
60-120ft
120ft+

151°40'E   151°50'E

7°30'N

7°20'N

7°30'N

Faneno
Fanangat
Fanos
Fanemoch
Winipires
Fano
Pisiras
Pisiwi
Airport
Weno
Ferit
Ette Mokumok
Eot
Udot
Oan
Param
Fanapanges
Tonoas
Fanamu
Eten
Oan
Totiu
Fefan
Uman
Siis
Fanannon
Fonou

Practicalities

Climate

Land temperatures on all the FSM islands average 84°F (28°C) year-round. Rainfall is heaviest on Pohnpei, whose interior gets a whopping 400 inches (1,016cm), though Kolonia gets less than half of that. The wettest months are generally October through December. The driest months are January and February. It is blustery during March and April when the northwesterly trade winds blow in; winds are calmest from June through September. Keep in mind that strong prevailing gusts may affect certain dive sites anytime, so it is good to check on this daily. The FSM islands are mostly outside the classic typhoon tracks, though they are not immune.

Year-round water temperature averages a balmy 80°F (27°C). Gin-clear waters make 100ft (30m) visibility the norm, although it can drop a bit in the mangroves.

Language

English is the official language for government, commerce and inter-island communications, although the islands have their own indigenous languages as well. On Chuuk it's Chuukese, but there are also several minority dialects. Many elderly people are fluent in Japanese, a holdover from pre-war years. On Pohnpei it's Pohnpeian, though Mokilese, Pingelapese, Ngatikese and Nukuoro-Kapingamarangi are also spoken; on Kosrae folks speak Kosraean.

Pohnpeian women work together weaving thatch for a new house roof.

Getting There

Travel to the FSM is available on Continental Airline's island-hopper via Hawaii and Guam three times weekly or, more frequently, from Manila and Japan via Guam. Continental is the only international carrier for Chuuk and Kosrae. Pohnpei is also served twice a week by Air Nauru, which flies to Nauru (with connections to Australia, Tarawa and Fiji) in one direction, and to Guam and Manila in the other.

Gateway City - Kolonia

Kolonia, the capital of Pohnpei, is the gateway to this region as it is served by airlines from all directions. Steeped in history, Micronesian and Polynesian culture, this warm town is well worth a visit.

Kolonia's airport sits at the end of a long peninsula leading to the harbor; the town is at the base of the peninsula. Its baseball field is a major gathering spot; the outfield "fence," an old 1899 Spanish wall complete with arched doorways and a stone façade, was once part of Fort Alphonso XII. Nearby, the small Lidorkini Museum has many informative cultural exhibits. Towering above the trees is the 1907 vintage German bell tower and a gravesite of Capuchin priests.

Many small stores sell colorful dresses, crafts, fresh fruit and $1 cheeseburgers. You'll find restaurants and two banks along the main street.

Learning Local Lingo

Chuukese Basics

Hello	ran annim	Please	kose mwochen
Goodbye	kone nom	Thanks	kilisou
How are you?	ifa usum?	(very much)	(chapur)
I'm well	ngang mei pochokum	Yes	wuu
(thanks)	(kilisou)	No	apw

Pohnpeian Basics

Hello/goodbye	kaselehie	Please	menlam
How are you?	ia iromw?	Thanks	kalangan
I'm well	i kehlail	Yes	eng
(thanks)	(kalangan)	No	soo

Kosraean Basics

Hello	lotu wo	Please	nunakmuna
Goodbye	kut fwa osun	Thanks	kulo ma lunhlhp
How are you?	kom fuhkah?	Yes	aok
I'm well	nga ku na	No	moohi

Also take a stroll into the Polynesian village of Porakiet, where craftsmen whittle necklaces from the local palm ivory nuts and fashion striking mangrove-wood sharks.

Flights to Chuuk and Kosrae leave from Kolonia regularly. You can fly directly to Chuuk from Guam, but a visit to rustic Kolonia is highly recommended.

Getting Around
Chuuk

Taxis on Weno are plentiful but may not be that recognizable. Practically every other car declares itself a "taxi" and the only identifying feature is a hand-printed cardboard taxi sign placed on the dashboards of pick-up trucks and cars.

Rental cars are also available. Your hotel can help arrange a rental car or try **Truk Stop Car Rentals** (☎ 330-4232). **Kurassa Apartments** (☎ 330-4415) also arranges car rentals. In downtown Weno, shops and restaurants are reasonably close, so cars are a convenience but not a necessity. Check with the dive shop or your hotel about any kind of shuttle service it may offer.

Local boats provide ferry services to the other islands where walking is the primary mode of transport, although there are a few taxi pick-up trucks on Tonoas.

Tourists take a local "taxi" tour of war remnants on Tonoas.

Pohnpei

Taxis are plentiful in the Kolonia area and can be called to most locations. Two popular companies include **Lucky 7** (☎ 320-5859) and **Waido** (☎ 320-5744). Drivers tend to drive like bats out of hell, so tell your driver to slow down if he starts to scare you. Rental cars are available at the airport and through hotels and can be useful—though not necessary—as Pohnpei has good roads around 70% of the island.

Kosrae

Taxis are available through **Thurston Taxi** (☎ 370-3991), Kosrae's only taxi service. Rental cars can be arranged through your hotel or at the airport, although you may not need one. Kosrae's dive operations provide shuttle service to the harbors, so you get to see a good slice of Kosraean life along the half-hour drive. Most people will eat at resort restaurants, so a rental car may be useful only on non-diving days and Sundays.

Entry

Each island airport has its own customs and immigration officers. If you plan on visiting several islands on one trip, you will be passing through customs and immigration lines at each stop and filling out paperwork. You automatically get a new entry permit, good for up to 30 days, each time you fly into a new district center. Entry permits can be extended through the immigration offices for up to 90 days, or up to 365 days for U.S. citizens.

U.S. citizens may enter any FSM state with a passport or proof of U.S. citizenship, such as a birth certificate. Non U.S. citizens must have a valid passport from their country of origin. Vaccination or certification is not required unless you are coming from an infected area. Plants and animals must be given prior approval before entry, and animals must be quarantined. Importation of controlled substances or weapons is prohibited. Every visitor must demonstrate the intent to travel onward beyond the FSM, such as a return ticket.

Each island has an airport departure tax, payable in U.S. dollars. In Chuuk it's $10, Pohnpei $15 and Kosrae $10. You need to pay this in cash—credit cards are not accepted.

Time

The FSM spans two time zones. Yap and Chuuk are 10 hours ahead of GMT; Pohnpei and Kosrae are 11 hours ahead. If it is noon in Chuuk it will be 1pm in Kolonia, noon in Sydney, 2am in London and 6pm the previous day in San Francisco.

Money

The U.S. dollar is the official currency throughout the FSM. Major credit cards are accepted at most visitor-oriented businesses, especially dive shops and high-end hotels. Try to bring U.S. dollars, as foreign currency exchange is a hassle. Automatic teller machines are few and prone to malfunction.

Electricity

Electricity is the same as on the U.S. mainland: 110/120V, 60 cycles, with two-pronged plugs. Adapters and converters aren't readily available for photographers with 220V systems, so bring your own if you need to convert.

Sippin' Sakau

Pohnpei is famous for its energetic dances and for the relaxing drink, sakau, a kava-like brew. You will often see pick-up trucks driving down the street, filled with large, green leafy plants whose long roots trail from the pick-up bed. These are pepper plants and their roots are destined to be pulverized and made into sakau.

Sakau pounders go to great ceremonial lengths. The roots are marginally cleaned and then taken to a special pounding stone made of basalt. The roots are thrashed until they become thin and pulpy. At major sakau ceremonies, teams of pounders compete to see who can get the job done first.

The metallic sound of the rocks hitting the basalt takes on a musical rhythm. The event unfolds at a frenzied pace, with the pounders hacking out a deafening song as people hoot, holler and dance. The pulverized root is then strained with water, resulting in a muddy-looking and muddy-tasting drink that acts as a mild narcotic, relaxing and even numbing the drinker. These sessions can go on all day with the participants becoming quite mellow by day's end. Tourists to Pohnpei can buy it by the bottle as it is made fresh in Porakiet. Drink it within six hours or it loses its potency.

Weights & Measures

The U.S. imperial system of weights and measures is used throughout the islands. All sale and rental dive gear is oriented this way—depths are measured in feet, weights in pounds and compressed air in pounds-per-square inch (psi). In this book, both imperial and metric measurements are given, except for specific references to depth within the dive site descriptions, which are given in feet. See the conversion chart in the back of this book for metric and imperial equivalents.

What to Bring

It never gets cold in FSM, but bring a light raincoat or a windbreaker for the boat, as a cool rain after a dive can be a bit chilly. Otherwise bring only light clothing. Attire is very casual and formal wear is considered unnecessary and impractical. (There was once a proposal to ban neckties from the FSM!) Hats, sunglasses and sunscreen are essential, especially on boats where you are particularly exposed to the sun's rays.

Most dive operators will check your C-card, so be sure to have it handy. If you are planning to rent gear, be sure to check availability ahead of time (see Diving Services in the Listings section).

The year-round water temperature is warm enough that you will need only a thin wetsuit or dive skin, mostly for protection against the occasional stings. The lagoons are rich in plankton and the odd nematocyst will sometimes zap a diver. The many jellyfish found on the Chuuk wrecks also sting, but are big enough to avoid.

Bring all vitamins and prescription drugs because there are no real pharmacies on the islands. Other basic food and health items are available in the local stores.

Underwater Photography

Film processing services are limited, and no camera sales or repair services are available. The live-aboards in Chuuk are well equipped for film processing, video playback and even some editing. Camera rentals are also limited to the live-aboards, although some dive shops have depth-tested point-and-shoot cameras. Batteries are available but are not always alkaline. The best bet is to be self-sufficient—bring plenty of your own film, batteries, converters and spare camera bodies and lenses.

Business Hours

Businesses are usually open weekdays from 8am to noon, and 1 to 5pm. On weekends most retail outlets are open but some have limited hours and are open only 8:30am to 1:30pm. Banking hours are weekdays 10am to 3pm, with some banks open later on paydays or Fridays. Banks and government offices are closed on weekends. Restaurants and bars are open nightly until 10pm, although bars sometimes stay open until midnight.

Telecommunications/Mail

The FSM enjoys modern, reliable telecommunication links worldwide. Fax and internet services are readily available at various FSM telecommunications buildings. Cost for internet use is $4 for the first hour, and $1 per 15 minutes after that.

Several newspapers (both government and private) are published, but the Pacific Daily News out of Guam is the only daily. Pohnpei and Chuuk have live satellite broadcasts of CNN and ESPN, available at most hotels and some bars.

U.S. postal rates apply. Post offices are open daily during regular business hours and are closed on weekends.

Accommodations

Chuuk

Chuuk has a number of small hotels, many of which commonly host divers. The largest is the **Blue Lagoon Resort** (☎ 330-2727). It sits on carefully manicured grounds and has Chuuk's only beachside accommodations, a dive shop, restaurant and dock. They can also arrange airport transportation.

Downtown, the **Christopher Inn** (☎ 330-2652) is known more as a business hotel, but divers stay there as well. The **Kurassa Apartments** (☎ 330-4415), out past the airport, has large rooms and airport pick-up can be arranged. The **Truk Stop Hotel** (☎ 330-2701) has good facilities for divers, including lockers and a pier for easy boat pick-up and drop-off.

Visitor hospitality is an honor in the FSM. Culturally speaking, tips are not expected, though wages are low in the FSM, so tipping is certainly appreciated.

Pohnpei

In Pohnpei, the **Village Hotel** (☎ 320-2797), with its thatched villas, caters to divers with its own dive center and has highly acclaimed cuisine. The **Pwohmaria Beach Resort** (☎ 320-5941) is quaintly rustic and convenient. It has a dive operation and is close to the boat docks.

South Park Hotel (☎ 320-2255) and restaurant is also popular with traveling divers although it has no dive operation. However, Kenny, the manager, is an instructor and can tell you a lot about various dive sites.

Other alternatives include **Yvonne's Hotel** (☎ 320-5130) and the **Cliff Rainbow Hotel** (☎ 320-2415). The **Penney Hotel** (☎ 320-5770) is across from the Pohnpei Visitors Bureau. The **Joy Hotel** (☎ 320-2447) is a pleasant town hotel with nicely furnished rooms.

The Village Hotel veranda on Pohnpei provides a relaxing retreat after diving.

Kosrae

Kosrae has a few hotels that pride themselves on catering to divers and all offer air-conditioned rooms. The **Kosrae Village Resort** (☎ 370-3483), a PADI 5-star facility, is set in a mangrove area with towering coconut palms and the beach is a stone's throw away. The thatched bungaloes were made out of local materials.

The Australian-run **Kosrae Nautilus Resort** (☎ 370-3567), also a PADI 5-star facility, is a few minutes' walk from the Lelu causeway. Its comfortable rooms sit just across the road from the white-sand beach and Blue Hole dive site.

Also popular, the **Sandy Beach Hotel** (☎ 370-3239), on the beach between Tafunsak and Lelu, has ocean-facing cottages, and the **Pacific Treelodge** (☎ 370-2102), half a mile north of Kosrae Nautilus Resort, has modern rooms in duplex cottages surrounding a mangrove pond.

Dining & Food

Most hotels and resorts have an attached or nearby restaurant, where you can get anything from local fish dishes to pizza. Weno is the only island in Chuuk that has restaurants—you cannot get food on the outer islands.

Local grocery and resort stores stock items like water, sodas, beer and snacks. Often your resort or dive operator will arrange for lunch.

The staple foods of the islands are breadfruit, rice, taro, yam, sweet potatoes and coconut. The main sources of protein are fish, crab, clams and pork. Some restaurants offer local fare on their menus.

Shopping

Chuuk

The stores in Weno offer a variety of goods including T-shirts with local expressions, handicrafts such as jewelry, carvings and love sticks. Carvers and weavers use pandanus and local woods to fashion wall mats, trays, fans, figures, war masks, dolphins, sharks, manta rays, turtles, love sticks and even shark-tooth studded war clubs.

Poke of Love

Chuukese love sticks are popular with the tourists, as their story is a good one. Back in the days of pandanu huts, every man had his own love stick that was uniquely carved so the woman of his choice would know it was his. At night, the man would slip the love stick through the hut and poke the woman. She could tell who it was by its feel. If she pulled it in, he could join her, if she wiggled it, she would come out to meet him. If she pushed it out, he was out of luck. Cement houses have put an end to the practice, but love sticks are still favorite Micronesian souvenirs.

Pohnpei

The people of the Porakiet area in Kolonia are from the atoll of Kapingamarangi and are world-famous for carving sea creatures from mangrove wood. They also carve palm ivory nuts, a unique locally grown woody substance that looks and feels like real ivory. They fashion these nuts into pendants of marine animals.

Many stores sell the local and pungent Pohnpei pepper. Although processed differently than in the past, the pepper is still quite zesty. Also look for locally processed copra products like coconut oil, shampoo, soap, and lotion. Coconut oil is especially good for your hair after a dive, to keep the sun and salt from drying it out.

Locals carve handicrafts such as these warrior heads.

Kosrae

The gift shops at Kosrae's resorts sell dive T-shirts, beach cover-ups, hats, etc. A Kapingamarangi carver in Tafunsak carves unique items out of mangrove wood. He is teaching local boys to carve as well, so see what they have come up with. Local stores sell staples like snacks and sodas.

Turtle & Black-Coral Products: To Buy or Not to Buy?

A few stores in the islands sell turtle and black-coral products. Although there is a legal turtle hunting season in the FSM, be aware before you buy turtle products that all eight species of the world's sea turtles are either endangered or threatened. Activities contributing to the demise of these creatures include: hunting for human consumption, production of turtle-shell jewelry and ornaments, loss of habitat because of tourism and development, and injury from ship propellers and boat traffic.

Also increasingly under pressure, black coral tends to grow in deep water and, because it is hard to get at, it is considered a somewhat valuable material. Appearing more golden than black underwater, when polished to a glossy black finish the coral is often fashioned into jewelry.

Unfortunately, black coral is still sold locally. Visitors can help discourage the depletion of wild black coral by taking only photographs and by not purchasing black-coral souvenirs.

Many countries do not allow the importation of turtle-shell or black-coral materials, so ask if you don't know what something is made of. Be sure to tell the store owner if you do not approve of the sale of products made from endangered species.

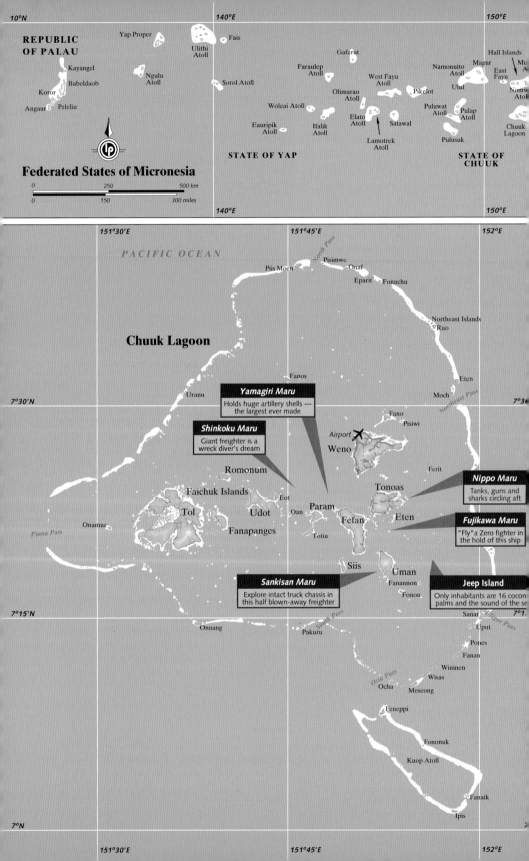

Federated States of Micronesia

REPUBLIC OF PALAU

Yap Proper
Ulithi Atoll
Fais
Kayangel
Ngulu Atoll
Babeldaob
Koror
Sorol Atoll
Angaur Peleliu

Gaferut
Faraulep Atoll
West Fayu Atoll
Namonuito Atoll
Magur
East Fayu
Mu
Hall Islands
Olimarao Atoll
Ulul
Pikelot
Nomw Atoll
Woleai Atoll
Puluwat Atoll
Pulap Atoll
Eauripik Atoll
Ifalik Atoll
Elato Atoll
Satawal
Pulusuk
Chuuk Lagoon
Lamotrek Atoll

STATE OF YAP

STATE OF CHUUK

| 0 | 250 | 500 km |
| 0 | 150 | 300 miles |

Chuuk Lagoon

PACIFIC OCEAN

Piis Moen
Pisimwe
Onaf
Eparit
Fonuchu
North Pass
Northeast Islands
Ruo
Fanos
Eten
Uranu
Moch
Northeast Pass

Yamagiri Maru
Holds huge artillery shells —
the largest ever made

Fano
Pisiwi

Shinkoku Maru
Giant freighter is a
wreck diver's dream

Airport ✈
Weno

Ferit

Romonum

Nippo Maru
Tanks, guns and
sharks circling aft

Faichuk Islands
Tonoas
Eot
Tol
Udot
Oan
Param
Eten

Fujikawa Maru
"Fly" a Zero fighter in
the hold of this ship

Onamue
Fanapanges
Totiu
Fefan

Piaan Pass

Siis
Uman
Fanannon

Sankisan Maru
Explore intact truck chassis in
this half blown-away freighter

Fonou

Jeep Island
Only inhabitants are 16 cocon
palms and the sound of the se

Onnang
Pakuru
Sanat
Uput
South Pass
Pones
Fanan
Wininen
Wisas
Ocha
Meseong
Otta Pass

Feneppi

Fononuk
Kuop Atoll

Fanaik
Ipis

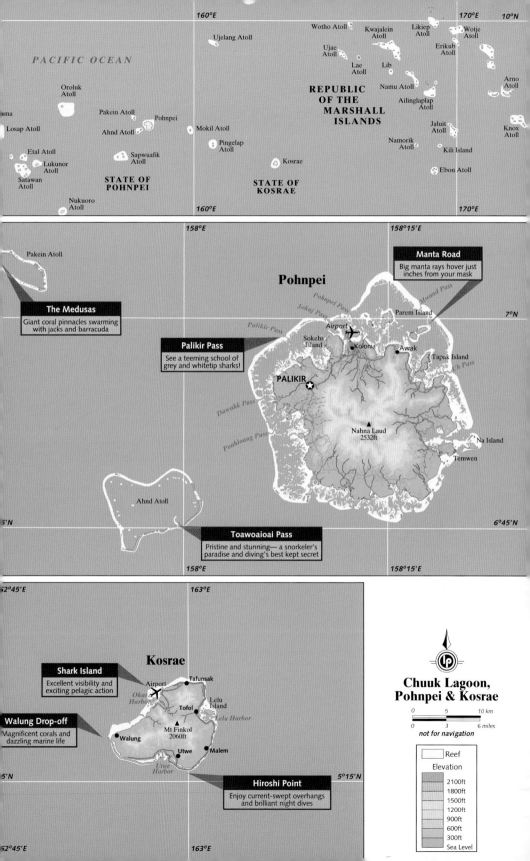

Map 1 (Top): Pacific Ocean / Republic of the Marshall Islands

PACIFIC OCEAN

160°E · 170°E · 10°N

Oroluk Atoll

ama

Losap Atoll

Pakein Atoll · Pohnpei

Ahnd Atoll

Etal Atoll

Lukunor Atoll

Satawan Atoll

Nukuoro Atoll

Ujelang Atoll

Mokil Atoll

Pingelap Atoll

Sapwuafik Atoll

STATE OF POHNPEI

Wotho Atoll · Kwajalein Atoll · Likiep Atoll · Wotje Atoll

Ujae Atoll

Lae Atoll

Lib

Namu Atoll

Ailinglaplap Atoll

Erikub Atoll

Arno Atoll

REPUBLIC OF THE MARSHALL ISLANDS

Namorik Atoll

Jaluit Atoll

Kili Island

Ebon Atoll

Kosrae

Knox Atoll

STATE OF KOSRAE

160°E · 170°E

Map 2 (Middle): Pohnpei

158°E · 158°15'E

Pohnpei

Pohnpei Pass

Mwand Pass

Jokaj Pass

Parem Island · 7°N

Palikir Pass

Airport

Manta Road
Big manta rays hover just inches from your mask

The Medusas
Giant coral pinnacles swarming with jacks and barracuda

Pakein Atoll

Palikir Pass

Sokehs Island

Kolonia

Awak

Tapak Island

Palikir Pass
See a teeming school of grey and whitetip sharks!

PALIKIR

Dawahk Pass

Nahna Laud 2532ft

Na Island

Temwen

Poahloong Pass

Ahnd Atoll

5'N · 6°45'N

Toawoaioai Pass
Pristine and stunning— a snorkeler's paradise and diving's best kept secret

158°E · 158°15'E

Map 3 (Bottom): Kosrae

52°45'E · 163°E

Kosrae

Tafunsak

Airport

Okat Harbor

Lelu Island

Tofol

Lelu Harbor

Shark Island
Excellent visibility and exciting pelagic action

Walung Drop-off
Magnificent corals and dazzling marine life

Walung

Mt Finkol 2060ft

Utwe

Malem

5'N · 5°15'N

Utwe Harbor

Hiroshi Point
Enjoy current-swept overhangs and brilliant night dives

52°45'E · 163°E

Map Legend

Chuuk Lagoon, Pohnpei & Kosrae

0 — 5 — 10 km
0 — 3 — 6 miles
not for navigation

Reef

Elevation
- 2100ft
- 1800ft
- 1500ft
- 1200ft
- 900ft
- 600ft
- 300ft
- Sea Level

Activities & Attractions

Chuuk

Wreck diving in Chuuk Lagoon means some deep dives and longer surface intervals (sometimes up to five hours) than reef diving normally dictates. Most people visiting the lagoon become hooked on the historical aspects of the islands. Moderate hikes and land tours are available and highly recommended. For history buffs, land tours of the islands show ruins that attest to the immense infrastructure that was needed to support the ships, planes and personnel the Japanese brought to Chuuk.

Weno

When visiting Chuuk, most tourists stay on Weno Island. The Chuuk Visitors Bureau, with its small but informative museum, is downtown near the harbor. Mt. Tonachao—recognizable by its single tree—overlooks the village.

The former Japanese communications center is now the high school. The huge, reinforced windows show the Japanese were somewhat prepared for, or at least expected, heavy battle.

Past the high school, a road winds through lush jungle and sandy shorelines to a trail that leads to the Weno lighthouse. The trail up provides steep views down the side of the mountain. You can climb up to the old lighthouse roof, where you get a good view of Chuuk Lagoon. Near the lighthouse are the remains of a Shinto shrine, and a large gun and bunker that make a modern-day playhouse for children.

Lagoon Islands
Tol

Tol is the highest island in the lagoon. It is part of a group of islands in the west lagoon known as the Faichuks, which are home to a third of Chuuk's population. If your diving takes you to the *Hanakawa Maru* or the Northwest Pass, you will be in the vicinity of Tol, which rises to 1,457ft (444m). A walk through Tol's jungles will take you past walls set in the mangroves, standing reminders of Japanese occupation. Little is left of the Japanese roads, but footpaths lead everywhere, including past the home of a local boat-building family who do their construction high in the mountains where air is cool and wood plentiful.

A channel created by the Japanese runs through solid rock, starting in the mangroves, past the Catholic church to the other side to Lemetol Bay, a place where sea turtles frequently graze on grasses.

Param

On Param, wrecked planes, targets of the U.S. air strike, were bulldozed off the end of the runway into the sea. These planes still sit partially out of the water. They are enclosed by a rock wall and are best observed from land. Snorkeling here is not advised because mangled plane parts can cause nasty cuts. Param was an auxiliary base of Eten (the main airstrip in the lagoon). Coconut trees and jungle cover most of what is left of the runway. The few residents here live a subsistence lifestyle by fishing, harvesting coconuts and making copra.

Tonoas

Tonoas (formerly "Dublon") was the main base for Japanese operations. Especially impressive are its melted-down fuel tanks, a deep freshwater reservoir and a system of caves carved into the hills, which once held hundreds of supply trucks.

This is a good place to get a glimpse of Chuukese life. A three-hour pick-up-truck tour is available through the Blue Lagoon Resort. Hardier types can also do the tour on foot. Either way, bring lots to drink.

Some of the sites to visit include the Japanese seaplane base, which is now the junior high school; a bunker and command post; the Admiral's House, which is now a Catholic mission where woven crafts are occasionally sold; the wartime communications center; General's Cave, a large cave that was used for bomb storage; the immense reservoir; and the hospital building. At the new dock check out the melted fuel tanks. They burned out of control for more than a week and now sit in the jungle like big, melted marshmallows.

Eten

Eten is a popular spot for lunch and between-dive decompression stops. The Zero fighter in shallow water at the northwest end makes for excellent snorkeling.

Eten was once a hotbed of Japanese wartime activity. Its past is still evident, although it is difficult to imagine the vast complex this island was in the days before the U.S. raids. Massive efforts by Japanese planners and local labor had transformed Eten (called "Take Jima" by the Japanese) into the largest airfield in Chuuk. The island's coastline was manually lined with basalt rock and filled with earth, forming an airstrip that was large enough to accommodate bombers. This feat was accomplished by Japanese, Korean, Okinawan and Chuukese workers starting in 1935. A taxiway led to two hangars, command buildings and barracks, underground stores and fuel tanks. This tiny island bustled with activity to support both air and sea movements—the Eten anchorage was also a primary staging area.

During the war, forced labor hand-built a seawall to extend the runway off Eten Island.

Eten was a major target of U.S. fighters and bombers. Strafings and bombings early on, including a direct hit to the headquarters building, cost many lives and made communication impossible when the Japanese tried to organize retaliatory forces. Large craters in the runway hampered take-offs and most of the planes were disabled.

Today, Eten is tranquil. The runways are overgrown with tapioca patches and banana plants. There are no roads, cars, or electricity. But the vestiges of past occupation are still apparent. Instead of housing the combatants and instruments of war, the wartime buildings fill a need on the island: one cement structure whose outer walls are riddled with bullets from the strafing attacks now holds pandanu branches that are cut and laid out to dry. These will later be used to make roofs, sleeping mats or carrying baskets. One building is used as a laundry, while another is used for coconut storage.

A long, steep climb to the top of Eten takes you to a promontory that overlooks the anchorage and a breathtaking view of the outer barrier reef. A large anti-aircraft gun sits on its mounts, well preserved despite its years of retirement.

Pohnpei

Hiking is especially rewarding in Pohnpei, where the large landmass opens up many avenues for exploration. **Waterfall hikes** can take five minutes or up to four hours, depending on the gusher you want to see.

Nan Madol is an ancient stone city built on 100 artificial islets off the southeast coast of the island. The ruins consist of immense basalt rock logs brought to the islands by raft (some say by magic) to construct steps, paths and a temple. The stone fortress was built on a reef southwest of Temwen Island, by the rulers of Pohnpei around 500 AD. Archaeologists and engineers are attempting to discover more about the people who constructed the island city, which remained under Pohnpei rule until it was taken over by Isokelekel, a warrior who installed the present traditional system in the 1520s.

Nan Madol is reached by boat from Kolonia, or by car. It's a full-day boat tour that usually includes a visit to the spectacular **Kepirohi Waterfall** and snorkeling inside the lagoon.

A 20-minute drive out of Kolonia takes you to a large natural pool where the river slows. Farther along the main road is the turn to the spectacular **Liduduniap Twin Waterfalls**. The viewing area has thatched huts where you can rest or picnic in a natural jungle setting. Pohnpei has several protected natural park and recreation areas, complete with waterfalls and swimming holes.

A daytrip to privately owned **Kephara (Black Coral) Island** offers beach relaxation and snorkeling. For a family day, visit **Langer Island**, which has

Mysteries of Nan Madol

Although Nan Madol is Pohnpei's foremost land attraction for foreigners, some Pohnpeians feel uncomfortable there—the local belief that people shouldn't disturb the ruins may be more than mere superstition. In 1907, Pohnpei's German governor died of a mysterious ailment immediately after excavating a burial tomb on Nan Madol. The German

administration claimed it was heat exhaustion but a lot of older Pohnpeians still doubt that diagnosis.

Nan Madol holds its mysteries well. Some believe that the legendary lost continent of Mu, or Lemuria, may lie off its waters and that Nan Madol was built as a mirror image of a sunken city, which at the time of construction, could still be seen lying beneath the water's surface.

Pohnpei's popular Kepirohi Falls is one of 42 waterfalls on this lush island.

simple cottages where you can stay overnight for a small fee. These trips can be arranged by resorts or diving services. Regardless of how you get there, be sure to bring mosquito spray.

Outer-island journeys are available via charter plane or government boat to Mwoakilloa, Pingelap, Nukuoro, Sapwuafik and Kapingamarangi. The boat schedules can mean weeks or months between trips, so staying on these islands is very difficult and requires the permission from the chiefs (which can be obtained beforehand from chief representatives in Kolonia or Palikir).

Not to be missed is **Sokehs Rock**, Pohnpei's boldest landmark. Guided hikes can be tailored to fit your level of fitness and interest. A guide can take you scaling on Sokehs's steep face, or you can arrange a mellow hike. The visitors bureau has a good list of tour companies.

Kosrae

If you're not in great shape or just short on time, there are some convenient sites to visit that don't require strenuous hiking. One such site on Kosrae is **Sipyen Waterfall**, which sits not far off the road up the Utwe River. A sign along the road indicates the semblance of a trail leading up to the falls, or you can take the easier route and head up the riverbed. Look for small, black tadpoles by the hundreds in the shallows, and for tiny fish and shrimp in the eddy pools. The falls empty into a cool pool that is great for sitting in, soaking up the roar of the falls and jungle sounds. Although the water looks clear and clean, do not drink it, as Kosrae has feral pigs whose droppings carry a parasite that can, if ingested through water, make humans quite sick. But the water is safe to swim and romp in.

For adventurous types, a hike up to **Mt. Omah** will take you high into the rainforest via a series of switchback trails clogged with towering vegetation. War caves are burrowed into the mountainside. The overlook on the way up shows the entire Malem coastline. The hike ends high up at a series of cascading waterfalls pouring through the upper jungle.

A local guide, Hamilson Phillip, lives at the base of this trail and accompanies everyone (from forestry officials to naturalists and historians) through the jungle. He is full of local lore and interesting tidbits, such as how natural eyewash can be garnered from the ginger plant. Hamilson doesn't have a phone, but your hotel will likely be able to find him.

On the west side of the island, you can explore the rich and incredibly thick mangroves at the **Walung Conservation Area** and **Trochus Reserve**. The hiking is guaranteed wet and a little rough as pointed mangrove roots poke through the soft silt bed. The vegetation in these natural enclaves is unique, with some species endemic to Kosrae. Towering trees with massive root systems form a canopy covering secluded trails, waterways and gentle lowland streams. At high tide, small boats can wind into the mangrove preserve. Native birds wing overhead and

Kosrae's rivers that flow from the mountains are bordered by lush jungle.

young marine fish and mudskippers dart through the maze of roots and fallen debris. Deep in the mangroves towering endemic *terminalia* trees, over 100ft (30m) high, are as straight as telephone poles. Their broad canopy shadows the fertile floor below.

At the other end of this vast reserve, on the northern mouth of the Finkol River, past the pleasant village of Utwe (also called Utwa) is the **Utwe-Walung Marine Park**. The visitors center has a wealth of information on the eco-system and occasionally hosts cultural shows. It can also arrange guided tours in outrigger canoes.

For a trip back in time, take a visit to the **Lelu Ruins**, where remnants of the royal city and feudal capital of Lelu still cover a third of the island. If you want to inspect the ruins by taking a ride around the perimeter of the island, forget it—the ruins are almost completely hidden behind the lush vegetation and a smattering of homes. This ancient fortress is best explored on foot. Inside the high basalt walls that enclose the various compounds, you'll see coral pathways, royal burial mounds and dwellings of various chiefs.

The **Kosrae State Museum**, nestled up on a hill near the government offices, has good information on the Lelu Ruins, along with artifacts collected by original European expeditions and early missionaries. The museum also has a large collection of videotapes documenting many facets of Kosraean life.

Kayaking in the dense, ancient mangroves is a unique way to explore the islands.

Kayaking

Kayaking is a relatively new sport to the islands but gaining in popularity, especially as more trained guides and quality kayaks are brought in. In Chuuk, kayaks can be rented at the Blue Lagoon Resort. Tours include gliding past war relics down the northwestern shore of Weno; checking out the seaplane base along southern Tonoas; and paddling through mangroves. In Pohnpei extensive kayaking itineraries include trips through the many mangrove areas, Nan Madol and through the Sokehs mangrove maze. Ask your hotel to contact avid kayaker and community college professor Howard Rice to arrange a trip. Howard teaches tourism and will gladly take you kayaking, or arrange for one of his students to take you out. Paddling through Kosrae's mangrove canopies and inshore rivers is truly awe-inspiring. Fiberglass kayaks are available at Kosrae Village Resort and most hotels can arrange for tours in local outrigger canoes. Timing is essential to safely enjoy the mangroves—make sure you start with the incoming tide.

Birding

Following winged creatures with binoculars or a camera can be very rewarding on these islands. Beautiful kingfishers, honeyeaters and heron are just some of the 200 or so bird species found in Micronesia. The Chuuk greater white-eye lives in the mountain jungles on Tol, where the restricted terrain serves as this bird's sole habitat. Ornithologists have set up camp on Tol to study birds, especially migratory birds that are reported to come from Asia. Pohnpei's state bird is a hyperactive little lorikeet. There are some elegant seabirds as well, like the white-tailed tropic birds that ride the upper currents along the Sokehs Rock cliff line. In Kosrae, shorebirds such as cranes and broad-footed plovers are plentiful and can be easily photographed.

Fishing

Yellowfin tuna, albacore, marlin, wahoo, mahi-mahi and rainbow runners are just some of the blue-water fish found off the shores of these islands. Most fishers still troll with handlines, which can be a real test of skill and strength if a marlin gets on the line. There are no major daily fishing operations in the islands, but most of the diving services can arrange an afternoon of trolling. Chuuk's best fishing is outside of the lagoon. Fishing and spearfishing on the wrecks is illegal, although the activity is nearly impossible to police—local spearfishers have harvested the larger fish from the wrecks anyway. Beware that the many sharks both inside and outside the lagoon aren't at all shy about challenging hunters for a speared fish. Spearing is best left to experienced locals.

Be sure there's a line in the boat when you visit Pohnpei's atolls. In Kosrae, fishing from the buoys is legal and it is easy to tie up and cast for fish. Ask your hotel to arrange for a guided fishing venture, as fishing is prohibited in some conservation areas.

A local fisherman shows off his day's catch.

Diving Health & Safety

General Health

The FSM is generally a healthy place to visit. There are no tropical diseases—unlike other areas in the South Pacific, malaria is not a threat here. Each of the FSM states has a major hospital where basic health care is available, but these are not well equipped for any serious medical complication. Be aware that the nearest major medical facilities are found in Hawaii and Manila.

Tap water is drinkable on some islands and at certain hotels, but it's always best to ask first. Bottled water is also readily available.

The U.S. Centers for Disease Control and Prevention regularly posts updates on health-related concerns around the world, specifically for travelers. Contact the CDC or visit their website: www.cdc.gov. Call (toll-free from the U.S.) ☎ 888-232-3299 and request Document 000005 to receive a list of documents available by fax.

Pre-Trip Preparation

Your general state of health, diving skill level and specific equipment needs are the three most important factors that impact any dive trip. If you honestly assess these before you leave, you'll be well on your way to assuring a safe dive trip.

If you're not in shape, start exercising. In Chuuk Lagoon, the deep diving and rides to the outer reef can be tough on your body. Take time to get in shape before your trip. Jet lag will be enough of a problem without adding poor physical conditioning to the equation.

Diving & Flying

Most divers in Chuuk Lagoon, Pohnpei and Kosrae arrive by plane. While it's fine to dive soon *after* flying, it's important to remember that your last dive should be completed at least 12 hours (some experts advise 24 hours, particularly after repetitive dives) *before* your flight to minimize the risk of decompression sickness, caused by residual nitrogen in the blood.

If you haven't dived for a while (six months is too long) and your skills are rusty, do a local dive with an experienced buddy or take a scuba review course. Feeling good physically, diving with experience and with reliable equipment will not only increase your safety, but will also enhance your enjoyment underwater.

At least a month before your trip, inspect your dive gear. Remember, your regulator should be serviced annually, whether you've used it or not. Be sure to change your dive computer battery or buy a spare to take along. Gear rental and servicing is limited in these islands. You might consider taking spare parts or even spare gear. A spare mask is always a good idea. Purchase any additional equipment you might need, such as a dive light and tank marker light for night diving, a line reel for wreck diving, etc. Make sure you have at least a whistle attached to your BC. Better yet, add a marker tube (also known as a safety sausage or come-to-me).

About a week before taking off, do a final check of your gear, grease o-rings, check batteries and assemble a save-a-dive kit. This kit should at minimum contain extra mask and fin straps, snorkel keeper, mouthpiece, valve cap, zip ties and o-rings. Don't forget to pack a first-aid kit and medications such as decongestants, ear drops, antihistamines and seasickness tablets. Be sure to fill any prescriptions before you leave, as there are no real pharmacies in Chuuk, Pohnpei or Kosrae.

Medical & Recompression Facilities

Exploring some shipwrecks in the Chuuk Lagoon necessitates very deep diving, well beyond sport diving limits of 130ft (40m). Only divers specially trained in deep diving should even consider venturing beyond these depths. There is no

Decompression Diving

While using a dive computer is a must while diving in Chuuk Lagoon, dive operators recommend a three-minute decompression stop at 15ft (4.6m) after all dives, even when your computer shows you are within no-decompression limits.

Divers exploring the deep wrecks will go into decompression during the dive. This means you will have to stop at the depths indicated on your computer upon ascent and before surfacing. A decompression stop (or "deco stop" in dive lingo) rids the body of excess nitrogen. Incomplete decompression can cause decompression sickness (DCS), more commonly known as "the bends."

To properly decompress, pay close attention to your computer, ascend slowly with at least a third or, even better, a half tank of air remaining. Stop at the level indicated, for the time indicated. Complete your decompression stop, slowly ascend, and then do another safety stop at 10 to 15ft (3 to 4.6m) for five minutes. Do not break your decompression, no matter what.

Repetitive decompression dives—anything more than one in 24 hours—are not recommended. Always make sure your dive boat has an emergency safety tank hanging for you at 20ft (6m). When unaccustomed to doing deep dives, many divers use more air on ascent than they bargained for. The emergency tanks ensure you have enough air to complete your safety stops.

recompression chamber in Chuuk, Pohnpei or Kosrae—the nearest chambers are on Guam, about a two-hour flight away. Dive conservatively—deep diving is not an activity to mess around with.

Technical diving services, such as nitrox and oxygen decompression stations (where an oxygen regulator is hung over the side of the boat, so divers can breath pure oxygen during a 15 to 20ft (4.6 to 6m) safety stop) are slowly being introduced in Chuuk. Check with your dive operator or live-aboard to see to what extent they offer these services.

Emergency Contacts

U.S. Navy Recompression Chamber (Guam)
COMNAVMARIANAS Dive Locker
☎ 671-339-7143 or ☎ 671-720-0342

Harmon Doctor's Clinic (Guam)
Dr. George Macris
☎ 671-637-1777 fax: 671-637-4385

FSM Medical Facilities
Chuuk's hospital is in Weno, near the government offices
☎ 330-2444 (emergency) or ☎ 330-2210 (non-emergency)

Pohnpei's hospital is on the main road, a mile from Kolonia
☎ 320-2213 (emergency) or ☎ 320-2215 (non-emergency)

Kosrae's small hospital is in Tofol
☎ 370-3333 (emergency) or ☎ 320-3012 (non-emergency)

DAN

Divers Alert Network (DAN) is an international membership association of individuals and organizations sharing a common interest in diving and safety. It includes DAN Southeast Asia and Pacific (DAN SEAP), an autonomous nonprofit organization based in Australia. DAN operates a 24-hour diving emergency hotline. DAN SEAP members should call ☎ 61 8 8212 9242. DAN America members should call ☎ 919-684-8111 or ☎ 919-684-4DAN (-4326). The latter accepts collect calls in a dive emergency.

Though DAN does not directly provide medical care, it does give advice on early treatment, evacuation and hyperbaric treatment of diving-related injuries. Divers should contact DAN as soon as a diving emergency is suspected.

DAN membership is reasonably priced and includes DAN TravelAssist, a membership benefit that covers medical air evacuation from anywhere in the world for any illness or injury. For a small additional fee, divers can get secondary insurance coverage for decompression illness. For membership questions, contact DAN at ☎ 800-446-2671 in the U.S. or ☎ 919-684-2948 elsewhere. DAN can also be reached at www.diversalertnetwork.org.

Diving in Chuuk Lagoon, Pohnpei & Kosrae

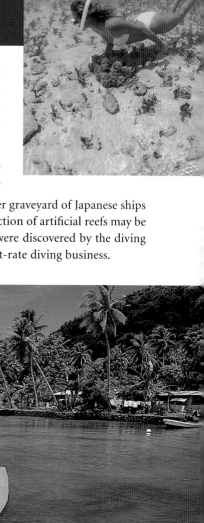

Chuuk Lagoon, Pohnpei and Kosrae offer a diverse range of natural ecosystems, from mangrove swamps to lush tropical rainforests and pristine coral reefs. Underwater naturalists, biologists and photographers will be awed by the species diversity in the nutrient-rich waters.

Chuuk Lagoon has more than 500 species of hard and soft corals, and over 700 different kinds of fish swim in and around the lagoon. The underwater graveyard of Japanese ships boasts over five decades of coral growth—this collection of artificial reefs may be the most beautiful in the world. Since the wrecks were discovered by the diving world in the late 1970s, Chuuk has developed a first-rate diving business.

STEFANIE BRENDL

A typical Chuuk Lagoon dive boat anchors off Eten Island.

47

About an hour's flight east of Chuuk and surrounded largely by rich mangrove forests and a vast outer barrier reef, Pohnpei's jagged coastline is intersected by numerous channels that carry nutrients into the vast lagoon. The island's hard coral reefs and colorful drop-offs are enchanting; rich lagoon waters attract the abundant marine life that makes Pohnpei one of the most varied marine environments in Micronesia. While shore diving and fishing off Pohnpei is superb, trips are also made outside of the barrier reef to two neighboring atolls, Ahnd and Pakein.

Less than an hour's flight southeast of Pohnpei, Kosrae is largely undeveloped and features some of the most pristine, lush and rugged terrain in all of Micronesia. Natural attractions are plentiful, making Kosrae excellent for outdoor enthusiasts.

Certification

While Open Water certification is available in all three locales, instructional courses are not heavily emphasized in either Chuuk or Pohnpei. In Kosrae, both the resorts—the Kosrae Nautilus Resort and the Kosrae Village Resort—offer all levels of instruction. A range of specialty courses is available at the Kosrae Village Resort, which is an IANTD technical diving facility and offers nitrox training. Confined-water training is done in a pool or in the natural swimming area near Lelu. Many shallow sites around the island make diving for beginners accessible and worthwhile.

Snorkeling

Nice patch reefs and beds of staghorn corals mean excellent snorkeling around many of Chuuk's inner-lagoon islands. Masts and cargo booms from some of the wrecks poke up near the surface. These pillars of life are covered with encrusting sponges, table corals, sea anemones and abundant tropicals, all of which can be easily observed while snorkeling. The outer-lagoon islands are also scenic with healthy, intact coral and white-sand floors.

In Pohnpei, the wonderfully clear water on the outer atolls makes snorkeling a delight, with 100ft (30m) visibility the norm. The inner-lagoon edges, and the tops of the channels and walls are all superb for tankless fun. At Manta Road, rays appear even when the high tide is slack. Snorkelers interested in the sea's more cryptic regions can explore the mangroves around Nan Madol and observe hiding juveniles.

Kosrae's fantastic mooring system gives anyone a chance to peer into the sea, even by just hanging from the back of the boat. The buoys are in fairly shallow water, but far enough away from the surf zone that snorkelers can swim near the boat without being tossed by surf. The water clarity makes a jump into the blue a great way to cool off, whether you have a tank on your back or not.

Inner reef and barrier reef passes provide clear snorkeling water and plenty of marine life.

Live-Aboards

Chuuk has three live-aboards that regularly ply its waters—the SS *Thorfinn*, the *Truk Aggressor II* and the *Truk Odyssey*. The *Thorfinn* uses a large, classic ship as a mother ship, which is basically a floating hotel. Boat tenders take small groups out to the dive sites. Dive times and locations are staggered, so only a few divers explore each wreck at a time. The *Thorfinn* normally anchors near Tonoas, but may move around during the week. Weekly or daily rates are offered. During calm summer months, the *Thorfinn* makes special trips to outer islands and atolls.

The *Truk Aggressor II* and the *Truk Odyssey* both take divers on 7-day trips, cruising to the most popular and interesting wrecks in Chuuk Lagoon. The staff on these boats were responsible for establishing the moorings found on most of the sunken ships. The moorings allow divers to enjoy repetitive dives, especially on the shallower wrecks, while the boat stays put. The *Aggressor* goes to the Solomon Islands part of the year, so check its annual schedule ahead of time (see the Listings section for contact information). The *Odyssey* runs trips year-round. Currently, no live-aboards visit Pohnpei or Kosrae.

Pisces Rating System for Dives & Divers

The dive sites in this book are rated according to the following system. These are not absolute ratings but apply to divers at a particular time, diving at a particular place. For instance, someone unfamiliar with prevailing conditions might be considered a novice diver at one dive area, but an intermediate diver at another, more familiar location.

The "Depth Range" given for each site refers to the depth the site is usually dived at. A "+" after the maximum depth indicates that the site has potential to go much deeper.

Novice: A novice diver should be accompanied by an instructor or divemaster on all dives. A novice diver generally fits the following profile:
◆ basic scuba certification from an internationally recognized certifying agency
◆ dives infrequently (less than one trip a year)
◆ logged fewer than 25 total dives
◆ little or no experience diving in similar waters and conditions
◆ dives no deeper than 60ft (18m)

Intermediate: An intermediate diver generally fits the following profile:
◆ may have participated in some form of continuing diver education
◆ logged between 25 and 100 dives
◆ dives no deeper than 130ft (40m)
◆ has been diving within the last six months in similar waters and conditions

Advanced: An advanced diver generally fits the following profile:
◆ advanced certification
◆ has been diving for more than two years; logged over 100 dives
◆ has been diving in similar waters and conditions within the last six months

Regardless of skill level, you should be in good physical condition and know your limitations. If you are uncertain as to your own level of expertise, ask the advice of a local dive instructor. He or she is best qualified to assess your abilities based on the prevailing dive conditions at any given site. Ultimately you must decide if you are capable of making a particular dive, depending on your level of training, recent experience and physical condition, as well as water conditions at the site. Remember that water conditions can change at any time, even during a dive.

Dive Site Icons

The symbols at the beginning of the dive site descriptions provide a quick summary of some of the following characteristics present at each site:

 Good snorkeling or free-diving site.

 Remains or partial remains of a wreck can be seen at this site.

 Sheer wall or drop-off.

 Deep dive. Features of this dive occur in water deeper than 90ft (27m).

 Strong currents may be encountered at this site.

 Strong surge (the horizontal movement of water caused by waves) may be encountered at this site.

 Drift dive. Because of strong currents and/or difficulty in anchoring, a drift dive is recommended at this site.

 Beach/shore dive. This site can be accessed from shore.

 Poor visibility. The site often has visibility of less than 40ft (12m).

 Caves are a prominent feature of this site. Only experienced cave divers should explore inner cave areas.

 Marine preserve. Special regulations apply in this area.

 Decompression dive. This site reaches depths that require single or multiple safety decompression stops.

As you fly in to Chuuk, the jet wings in over a breathtaking lagoon bordered by a surf-framed barrier reef. Green islets dot the seascape and peaks rise from the sea. A narrow airstrip protrudes and the plane makes a seemingly impossible landing. From the air, Chuuk Lagoon is unforgettable.

On land, Weno's busy port, where all of the commerce and business for the lagoon take place, seems a bit dirty and rundown. One must remember that Chuuk is not a wealthy state and the FSM is not a wealthy nation. The town's bumpy roads are a reminder that the U.S. left little infrastructure behind and that the state has been dismally unsuccessful at adding to what it inherited. Thus, at first glimpse, Chuuk is either bustling, colorful and rustic or simply dirty, run-down and poor.

In reality, Weno and all of the inner-lagoon islands are a real pleasure once you get to know the people and their culture. The islanders' relaxed Micronesian lifestyle will become quickly apparent. Chuukese dress colorfully and smile easily. Their houses are generally well kept, with flowering bushes and neat paths leading to their modest homes. Life is centered around the home and family.

Hotels catering to divers are clean and tidy. The many historic sites and laughing children of the other tranquil inner-lagoon islands make visits photogenic, fun and fascinating.

STEFANIE BRENDL

Aerial view of Eten, Tonoas and Weno Islands.

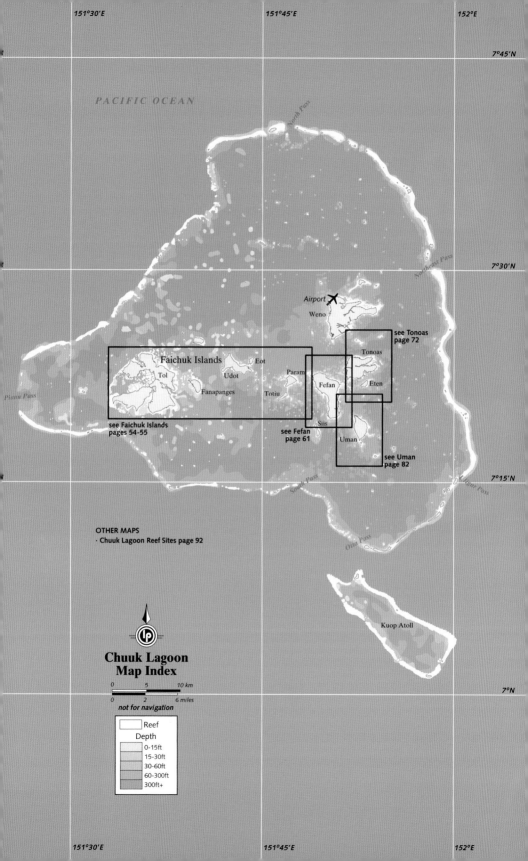

PACIFIC OCEAN

North Pass

Northeast Pass

7°45'N

7°30'N

Airport

Weno

see Tonoas
page 72

Faichuk Islands

Eot

Tonoas

Udot

Param

Eten

Tol

Fefan

Fanapanges

Totiu

Piaau Pass

see Faichuk Islands
pages 54-55

Siis

see Fefan
page 61

Uman

see Uman
page 82

7°15'N

South Pass

Otta Pass

Uigar Pass

OTHER MAPS
· Chuuk Lagoon Reef Sites page 92

Kuop Atoll

7°N

**Chuuk Lagoon
Map Index**

0   5   10 km

0   2   6 miles

not for navigation

Reef

Depth

0-15ft

15-30ft

30-60ft

60-300ft

300ft+

151°30'E

151°45'E

152°E

Chuuk Lagoon Shipwrecks

In the more than 50 years since most of the ships sank, their decks and sides have transformed into vibrant coral reefs. Each of the Chuuk Lagoon wrecks has everything a full-blown coral reef has, from pelagic predators like grey reef sharks, to colorful coral, reef fish and cleaning stations.

Many components must work together to make a healthy reef system thrive. The lagoon is full of nutrients that feed fish, anemones and corals. It is large enough that strong and constant currents carry these nutrients from the scattered islands through the large channels and out to sea. Many of the wrecks were sunk in or near the channels, where a wide variety of marine life thrives.

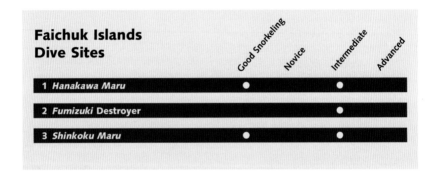

Faichuk Islands Dive Sites	Good Snorkeling	Novice	Intermediate	Advanced
1 *Hanakawa Maru*	●		●	
2 *Fumizuki* Destroyer			●	
3 *Shinkoku Maru*	●		●	

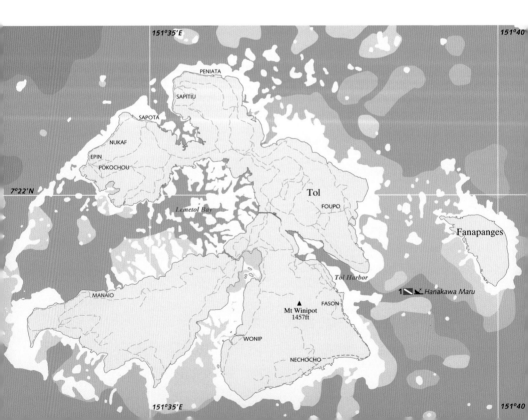

When visiting the wrecks, take a few minutes to simply stop and watch the activity going on around you. Not only are the wrecks incredible historic vestiges of the past, they are also some of the most complete and compact coral reefs found anywhere in the world.

Chuuk generally attracts more-experienced divers; the wrecks are mostly deep dives. A computer is recommended at all sites, as getting into a decompression situation is easy when doing multiple wreck dives. The ships are also silty, because they sit in the rich lagoon. It is best to dive only with divers who are trained and experienced in the lagoon's waters and wrecks.

In this section, for organization and mapping purposes, the Chuuk Lagoon shipwreck dives are broken up into four areas: Faichuk Islands (Tol, Udot and Param); Fefan; Tonoas; and Uman.

Dive the wrecks with experienced local divers.

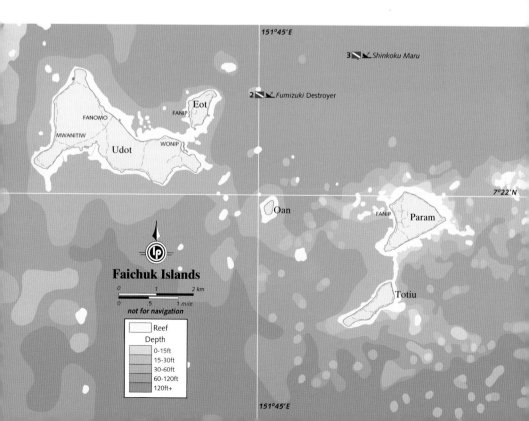

1 Hanakawa Maru

On a sunny day, the ride out to Tol in the Faichuk Islands is more than just a shuttle to a dive site. Locals fish in waist-high water using age-old methods and young men paddle small outriggers. The azure tones of the sea, lush greenery and billowing clouds around these many islands provide a feast for the eyes.

For nearly 50 years, the *Hanakawa Maru* was off-limits to divers. Something in the holds—possibly a petroleum product—was leaking from the ship and caused severe skin burns. That problem, combined with the journey to Tol—an hour's ride by speedboat from Weno—left the ship nearly untouched.

In 1990, the ship was determined safe and is now an ideal dive, although still

Location: Near Tol Harbor

Depth Range: 25-110ft (8-34m)

Access: Boat/Live-aboard

Expertise Rating: Intermediate

rarely visited. The masts and kingposts come close to the surface and support a nice collection of sea life. The ship sits on a slope. Its depth is about 50ft at the bridge, 80ft at the deck, and 100ft at the holds. The bow is shallower than the stern, which sits at about 110ft.

The ship is decorated with one of the most beautiful coral displays in Chuuk. Soft tree corals in all hues, sea fans, whips, black corals and tubastrea corals form lush growth. The bow is adorned with hard and soft corals, and multi-colored crinoids. A large anemone with colorful clownfish adorns a cargo derrick.

In the forward hold you'll find metal barrels (50-gallon drums) and what appear to be sandbags. The second hold features bent, jagged metal and a gaping hole caused by a fierce torpedo explosion. It is possible to swim from the second hold into the first via this damage hole, which is covered in sea life and gorgonian fans. Be careful not to harm these large gorgonians.

Many of the drums were emptied but apparently have air left inside. They sit pinned at the top of the holds in kind of an eerie defiance of gravity. There are also a couple of soyu (Japanese for "soy sauce") bottles doing the same thing in the bridge. The drums may have held the suspect petroleum products and

Fuel barrels in the *Hanakawa*'s forward hold.

may still be capable of leaking, so explore the holds with extreme caution. The substance that causes the burns has a reported milky appearance.

Enter the bridge from the hold or from above. It is well-lit and fun to explore, but it is very silty. Use caution to avoid a silt-out. Also look out for ceiling planks that appear to be rotting and falling on the lower level of the bridge. Take caution not to dislodge or snag equipment on these boards.

The skylight window glass over the engine room is still intact but the doors are heavily overgrown in coral and are a little tough to get through. Try entering from the west side if you intend to go in. Look for an army Howitzer gun aft and a rudder and four-bladed propeller over the stern.

2 *Fumizuki* Destroyer

When the *Fumizuki* was first discovered in April of 1987, the ship attracted a lot of attention. To find a new ship, especially a destroyer, within relatively easy diving depths was great news to both wreck divers and history buffs.

The *Fumizuki*, built in 1926 as a Mutsuki-class destroyer, eluded searchers for many years. Efforts to find the *Fumizuki* were spearheaded by Tomoyuki Yoshimura, a Japanese photographer and

Location: Near Udot

Depth Range: 80-120ft (24-37m)

Access: Boat/Live-aboard

Expertise Rating: Intermediate

journalist, and local dive authority Kimiuo Aisek. But searches in 1982 and

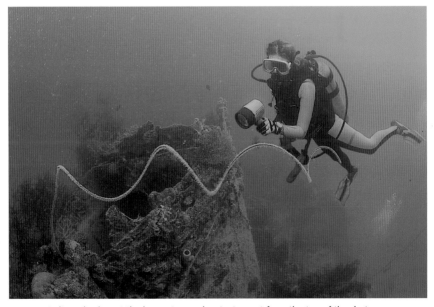

A diver checks out the long wire coral springing out from the top of the destroyer.

'86 failed. Finally Yoshimura placed an ad in a major Japanese newspaper, explaining that he was looking for surviving crew members. Amazingly, four men responded. The veterans' recollections lead to the *Fumizuki*'s discovery. The survivors' stories explained that the ship was in the midst of repair when the attacks started.

This is a beautiful wreck that is small enough to explore in one dive. It is covered with superb marine growth including soft corals, wire corals and fans. The ship sits upright with a slight list to port. The bridge is in about 90ft and the deck lies between 100 and 115ft. It has a big bow gun and a small stern gun that no longer has its barrel. The torpedo tubes are empty (and appear to have been brand new), the machine gun barrels are also off the guns, and there are no depth charges at the stern.

The ship is narrow with only a 30ft beam, so getting inside the engine room is tricky and not advisable. The ship is in good shape even though the bridge collapsed shortly after the wreck's discovery. Some plates and other artifacts are on display forward of the bridge— check out the goby living in one of the teapots. A human jawbone sits stashed by the engine room door—perhaps belonging to one of the four people who reportedly died in the engine room of this ship.

Damages are aft. The twin propellers at the rear of the ship are worth a look as they are large and overgrown with sessile marine life. Around the ship longnose barracuda and schooling mackerel hover above the seafloor.

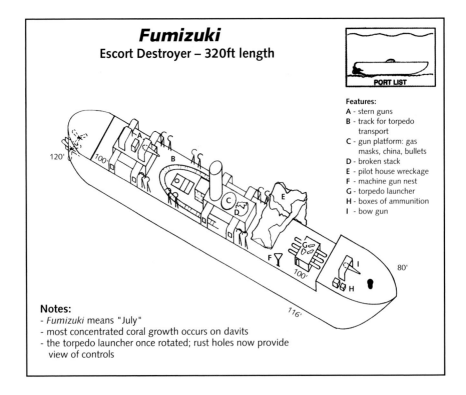

Fumizuki
Escort Destroyer – 320ft length

PORT LIST

Features:
A - stern guns
B - track for torpedo transport
C - gun platform: gas masks, china, bullets
D - broken stack
E - pilot house wreckage
F - machine gun nest
G - torpedo launcher
H - boxes of ammunition
I - bow gun

120' 100' 80' 100' 116'

Notes:
- *Fumizuki* means "July"
- most concentrated coral growth occurs on davits
- the torpedo launcher once rotated; rust holes now provide view of controls

3 *Shinkoku Maru*

Launched by the Kawasaki Dockyard in 1939, the *Shinkoku Maru* was outfitted as a heavily armed fleet oiler and became part of the initial striking force under Admiral Nagumo, whose attack on Pearl Harbor triggered the Pacific conflict.

Location: North of Param

Depth Range: 40-130ft (12-40m)

Access: Boat/Live-aboard

Expertise Rating: Intermediate

Most of its duty was in the Indian Ocean, and between Japan and Chuuk or Palau. An American torpedo struck it in August 1942, but it limped back to Chuuk for repair and was underway again in October. It sank while at anchor in Chuuk, after being struck by an Avenger bomber. An explosion and flash fire killed many crewmen; others drowned as the ship was quickly pulled under from the weight of the water-filled aft.

The ship is, without a doubt, one of the most popular and beautiful wrecks in the lagoon. It is a must-see, as it has just about everything a wreck diver hopes for: artifacts, great coral growth, excellent fish life and a manageable diving range. The *Shinkoku Maru* is a large freighter about 500ft long, so plan at least two dives to see it properly. It rests where the currents run through the lagoon, so the surrounding sea life is prolific. Shark observation is excellent, with grey reef and whitetip sharks swimming in the currents off both the bow and midships. Dogtooth tuna also course by. The bow is covered with soft, hard and leather corals, which are normally seen with their polyps extended for feeding. Both wide-angle and macrophotography are good here and night diving is excellent. The whole bridge area is covered in soft corals and other colorful invertebrates.

The midship superstructure is worthy of exploration. It contains a galley, where plates and cooking utensils are still visible. Marine worms have eaten the wooden cupboards. There is also a medical clinic with an operating table on which local guides have placed numerous medical supplies. There are blankets buried in the silt on the floor.

A surgeon's table holds artifacts from the *Shinkoku's* ward.

Nearby is the officer's bath with tile tubs and faucet intact.

The pipe bridge extends all the way back and is covered in coral growth. On the port side of the engine room, a big hole filled with twisted metal leads to the open ocean. This is where the ship took the hit that sunk it.

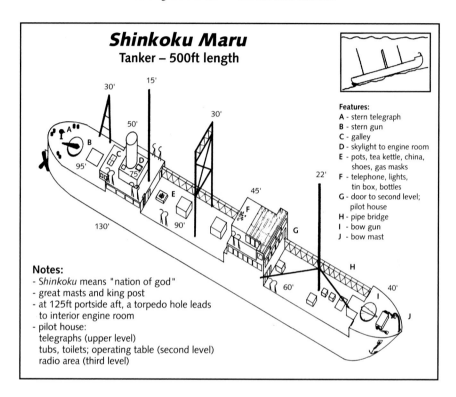

Shinkoku Maru
Tanker – 500ft length

Features:
A - stern telegraph
B - stern gun
C - galley
D - skylight to engine room
E - pots, tea kettle, china, shoes, gas masks
F - telephone, lights, tin box, bottles
G - door to second level; pilot house
H - pipe bridge
I - bow gun
J - bow mast

Notes:
- *Shinkoku* means "nation of god"
- great masts and king post
- at 125ft portside aft, a torpedo hole leads to interior engine room
- pilot house:
  telegraphs (upper level)
  tubs, toilets; operating table (second level)
  radio area (third level)

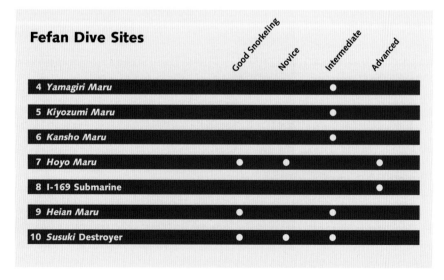

Fefan Dive Sites	Good Snorkeling	Novice	Intermediate	Advanced
4 *Yamagiri Maru*			●	
5 *Kiyozumi Maru*			●	
6 *Kansho Maru*			●	
7 *Hoyo Maru*	●	●		●
8 *I-169 Submarine*				●
9 *Heian Maru*	●		●	
10 *Susuki Destroyer*	●	●	●	

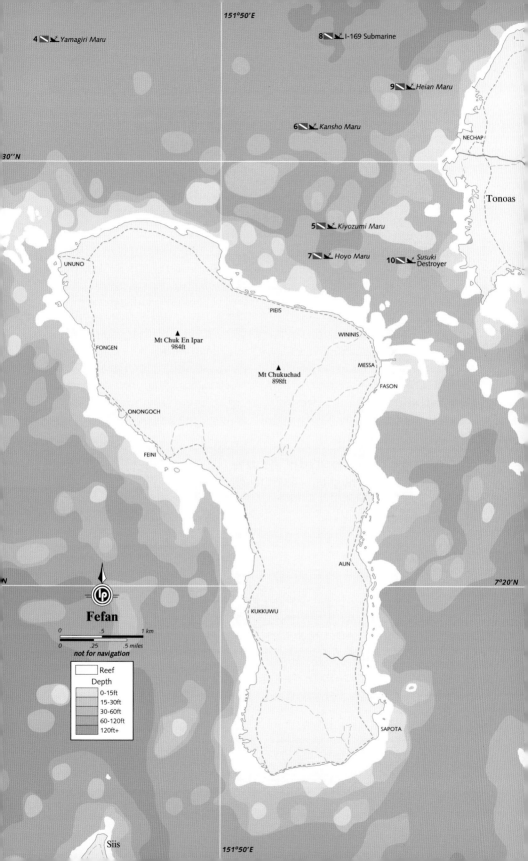

4 🏴⚓ *Yamagiri Maru*

8 🏴⚓ I-169 Submarine

151°50'E

9 🏴⚓ *Heian Maru*

6 🏴⚓ *Kansho Maru*

NECHAP

30''N

Tonoas

5 🏴⚓ *Kiyozumi Maru*

7 🏴⚓ *Hoyo Maru*   **10** 🏴⚓ *Susuki* Destroyer

UNUNO

PIEIS

WININIS

FONGEN

Mt Chuk En Ipar
984ft

MESSA

Mt Chukuchad
898ft

FASON

ONONGOCH

FEINI

AUN

7°20'N

Fefan

KUKKUWU

0   .5   1 km
0   .25   .5 miles
not for navigation

Reef
Depth
0-15ft
15-30ft
30-60ft
60-120ft
120ft+

SAPOTA

Siis

151°50'E

4 Yamagiri Maru

If you've seen photos of huge artillery shells taken in Chuuk, it is a pretty safe bet they were taken on the *Yamagiri*. The huge 18-inch artillery shells were destined for the guns of the battleships *Yamato* and *Musashi* but, before the *Yamagiri* could deliver, she was hit repeatedly during the air strikes over the lagoon. The ship caught fire and appears to have gone down slowly, now resting at about 110ft. This ship was the first found in Chuuk in the late '60s by a diver who noticed the different water color over the wreck.

Heavy coral growth decorates the stern, including a hot pink anemone, large barrel sponges and lots of cyan tube sponges. The *Yamagiri* rests on its port side and has a small gun on its forecastle. Most divers head to the impressively

Location: Northwest of Fefan

Depth Range: 50-110ft (15-34m)

Access: Boat/Live-aboard

Expertise Rating: Intermediate

large shells in the fifth hold. If you're photographing them, it pays to get into the hold first as silt kicks up easily.

The three forward holds are empty. You can enter the bridge through the third hold, which was hit hard—its steel girders are twisted like pretzels and the hole is big enough to easily swim through.

The bridge is an excellent site for photographing clouds of tiny baitfish

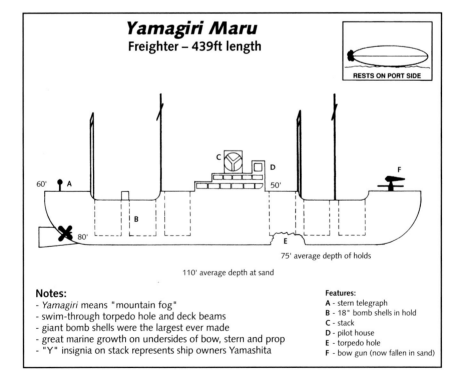

Yamagiri Maru
Freighter – 439ft length

RESTS ON PORT SIDE

60' A

C
D
F

50'

B

80'

E

75' average depth of holds

110' average depth at sand

Notes:
- *Yamagiri* means "mountain fog"
- swim-through torpedo hole and deck beams
- giant bomb shells were the largest ever made
- great marine growth on undersides of bow, stern and prop
- "Y" insignia on stack represents ship owners Yamashita

Features:
A - stern telegraph
B - 18" bomb shells in hold
C - stack
D - pilot house
E - torpedo hole
F - bow gun (now fallen in sand)

that nestle in some white coral trees. Inside the bridge, the portholes make fine photo subjects as they are covered with encrusting sponges, hydroids and other marine life. They still let in some daylight, but a dive light is needed while twisting through this area. The ship's telegraph is also located here.

If you want to avoid the crowd at the big shells, start at the forward damage hole and swim down the side. The hole is exquisitely decorated with gorgonians and fans, leather corals and beautiful, snowy white hydroids living in encrusting sponge communities. The coral life is excellent all over this ship. Under the bow you'll usually find a large school of batfish that will let you get within photo distance if you're careful. They are curious fish by nature and will come quite close. They are also highly reflective, so power down your strobe. The underside of the bow is beautiful, with ropes of hydroids growing everywhere. The bow gun is worth some photos as it is well-encrusted with corals. It fell off the ship in the mid-'90s and rests on the seafloor next to the ship.

Rope sponges surround a gas mask found on the *Yamagiri Maru.*

5   Kiyozumi Maru

This ship went down quickly after taking severe hits and now rests on its port side at 100ft. The first hold is plated over, but the second one is open, revealing bicycles hanging from the bulkhead. The bikes are now pretty deteriorated, but one is still partially intact and makes an interesting photo subject. The next hold has a huge propeller blade and a cargo of oil drums. The blades are over 6ft long and are an impressive sight.

The engine room is wide-open but dark, so bring a light. The catwalks and huge engine cylinders are all clearly visible. The next hold is the quickest way to get from one side of *Kiyozumi*

Location: North of Fefan

Depth Range: 40-105ft (12-32m)

Access: Boat/Live-aboard

Expertise Rating: Intermediate

to the next, as there is a massive torpedo hole that opens to the sea. It is overgrown with sea whips and black corals—swimming through it can be a surreal experience.

Eight gun platforms sit on the deck but only anti-aircraft guns remain. The ship has heavy marine growth in places, making some objects hard to recognize. A large anemone lives midship and schooling fish are common along the starboard side. Sea turtles occasionally rest on this ship, so look for them on the cargo booms and other extensions.

A lot of artifacts were removed from the ship and put on display. On the upper starboard deck, you'll see a large and heavy brass lantern, a medicine chest, some bottles, binoculars, brass door-knobs, plates and cups. Below, on the bridge, which is an open and easy swim-through, are more cups and plates, sake bottles and doorknobs. Inside the first forward hold hangs a former wooden footlocker with its contents of clothing and shoes spilled into the hold.

This ship got around. Within a year, this heavily used troop-transport ship was in Saipan, at the Battle of Midway, in Guam and then Rabaul in Papua New Guinea. It was headed for Chuuk in January 1944 when it was hit and damaged badly by an American sub. The *Kiyozumi* managed to get to Chuuk and was being repaired when she finally sank during the American carrier strikes. Helpless, it went down at a repair anchorage north of Fefan Island.

A lantern encrusted with corals on the *Kiyozumi*.

6 Kansho Maru

The *Kansho Maru* sits upright with a slight list to port and is shallow by most wreck-diving standards, giving divers more time to explore. It lies close to the main traffic lane off Fefan. The ship apparently went down after being struck by a torpedo at the first hold. The ship buckled and the keel is probably broken, although it's too hard to get at to confirm.

The main engine room skylights are open on this ship, allowing divers easy access. It is dark (at about 90ft) and a light is definitely handy. You can see two sets of three cylinders and part of

Location: North of Fefan

Depth Range: 25-130ft (8-40m)

Access: Boat/Live-aboard

Expertise Rating: Intermediate

the diesel engine, along with other odds and ends.

It doesn't take long to stir things up. Rainwater run-off deposits a silt covering on the ship, lowering visibility a little. If you want a scatter-free photo, get there first and move gently. The slight silt inconvenience aside, this wreck boasts large growths of soft corals, sponges, hard corals and calcareous algae.

Many of the artifacts are still intact on the *Kansho*. Various rooms feature items like high-powered binoculars, a sextant and deer antlers. Bottles and plates are also common. You can see remnants of medical tables (or possibly beds) inside one of the bridge decks. The holds contain an assortment of interesting cargo, including a stack of old bicycles in the fifth hold. Check out the galley aft—it appears to be ready for someone to start cooking a meal, with plates and bottles on display.

The *Kansho*'s open engine room is ripe for exploration.

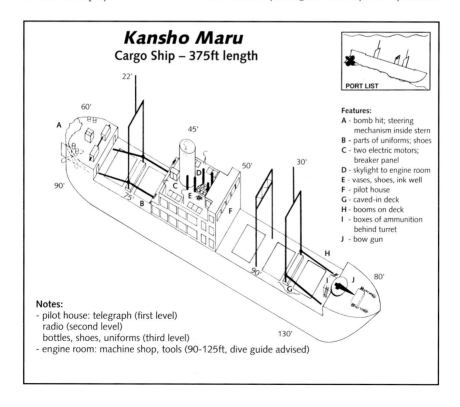

Kansho Maru
Cargo Ship – 375ft length

PORT LIST

Features:
A - bomb hit; steering mechanism inside stern
B - parts of uniforms; shoes
C - two electric motors; breaker panel
D - skylight to engine room
E - vases, shoes, ink well
F - pilot house
G - caved-in deck
H - booms on deck
I - boxes of ammunition behind turret
J - bow gun

Notes:
- pilot house: telegraph (first level)
  radio (second level)
  bottles, shoes, uniforms (third level)
- engine room: machine shop, tools (90-125ft, dive guide advised)

7 Hoyo Maru

When you first look at the *Hoyo Maru* it appears to be a coral reef. It is, in fact, a large (470ft-long), upside-down tanker built in 1936 by Mitsubishi. Besides the great variety of hard-coral growth and the dazzling antics of the sapphire damselfish that form clouds over the hull, there is much to see on this wreck, though it may not be immediately obvious.

It sits on an undersea hill and starts in only 10ft, but slopes all the way down to 120ft. The superstructure midship keeps the ship from touching the seafloor, so you can explore it by swimming under the large clearance between the sand and ship's deck. This feat is not for the claustrophobic (the ship is 60ft wide). Some algae, encrusting growth and whip corals grow underneath, but fin gently as the bottom stirs up easily.

In many areas, black-coral growth provides refuge for small baitfish. Fluted oysters also inhabit the wreck's walls.

Location: North of Fefan

Depth Range: 10-120ft (3-37m)

Access: Boat/Live-aboard

Expertise Rating: Novice (shallow); Advanced (deep)

The hull is cracked and, at about midship along the top, lace corals have formed through a hole where water gently rushes with the surge. This delicate growth looks like it was planned by some underwater architect and doesn't grow on many other wrecks in Chuuk.

This makes a good dusk dive. You can go down deep and swim under the ship, and then can come up shallow and wait for the brilliant yellow tube coral polyps and the multi-colored crinoids to come out as night sets in.

8 I-169 Submarine

Found in 1973, the I-169 is almost a novelty dive as it is deep and not that

Location: Northwest of Tonoas

Depth Range: 65-125ft (20-38m)

Access: Boat/Live-aboard

Expertise Rating: Advanced

A crew error left American sailors trapped beneath the I-169's now-open hatch.

large, so it doesn't take long to see. This American sub sunk accidentally, prior to the April 1944 U.S. bomber air strike. It dived underwater to avoid the bombs, but someone on the crew had failed to close the main induction valve, flooding the sub. The crew managed to stay alive for a couple of days, but perished after failed rescue attempts. The Japanese later blasted the front of the sub with depth charges, apparently so the Americans couldn't salvage the ship.

A lot of sessile marine life grows on the wreck. One hatch is now propped open; however, you should not penetrate the sub. It is too tight inside for the average diver and there isn't much left to see. The sailors' remains have long since been removed.

The aft conning tower is the highest part of the sub and is a haven for marine life, including streaming whips and a hovering cloud of tiny baitfish.

Baitfish swarm around the I-169's conning tower.

9 Heian Maru

This ship was made famous by Jacques Cousteau when his divers showed film footage of the ship's English and Japanese names still intact and readable on the bow. The *Heian* carried supplies for Japanese submarines, and periscopes line the upper passageway. This is a long swim-through, brightened with streaming shafts of light.

Ammunition still sits in the small aft hold. Near the bridge a fine assortment of artifacts from the galley are on display for divers to see, including a porcelain water dispenser, teacups and plates.

A great deal of fish life resides on this ship, making it a good photographic

Location: Northwest of Tonoas

Depth Range: 40-105ft (12-32m)

Access: Boat/Live-aboard

Expertise Rating: Intermediate

site. In the passageways, schools of small fish gather, parting just inches from your mask as you swim through. Look for juvenile marine life, including tiny lizardfish. There is some coral growth but not as prolific as on other shallower wrecks.

Look for the words "Heian Maru" on the bow of this ship.

A diver inspects galley items on display in the *Heian*.

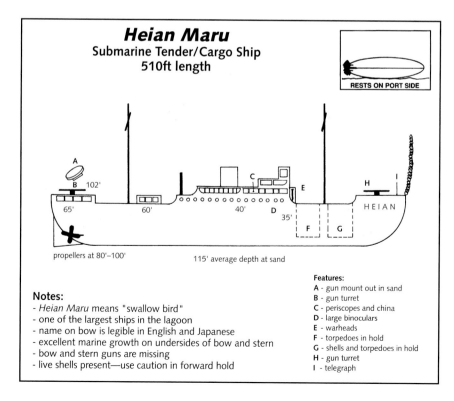

Heian Maru
Submarine Tender/Cargo Ship
510ft length

RESTS ON PORT SIDE

A
B   102'
65'   60'   40'   D
                              35'
E
H   I
HEIAN
F   G

propellers at 80'–100'   115' average depth at sand

Notes:
- *Heian Maru* means "swallow bird"
- one of the largest ships in the lagoon
- name on bow is legible in English and Japanese
- excellent marine growth on undersides of bow and stern
- bow and stern guns are missing
- live shells present—use caution in forward hold

Features:
A - gun mount out in sand
B - gun turret
C - periscopes and china
D - large binoculars
E - warheads
F - torpedoes in hold
G - shells and torpedoes in hold
H - gun turret
I - telegraph

The *Oite*'s Bad Timing

The *Oite* destroyer, a deep, only occasionally visited wreck just inside the North Pass, was simply in the wrong place at the wrong time. The ship left Chuuk February 16, 1944, as an escort to the *Agano*, a light cruiser. A sub chaser also joined them. The convoy was about 200 miles northeast of Chuuk when the U.S. submarine Skate torpedoed the *Agano* at dusk. The two escort ships took the *Agano*'s men—450 went aboard the *Oite*, packing the tiny destroyer to the hilt.

The *Agano* sank at about noon the next day. That afternoon, while the air strikes were underway, a radio message was sent to the *Oite* requesting its return to Chuuk to help engage enemy ships. Although the *Oite* was virtually defenseless—it was on its way to be refitted in Japan, and had little in the way of weapons or ammunition—it turned around and steamed back to the lagoon.

Of course, it wasn't long before it was engaged, first by U.S. Hellcats and then by Avengers. In the end, a torpedo from one of the planes hit aft of the bridge, splitting the ship into two pieces as it sank, causing one piece to capsize while the other remained upright.

Few people survived. Bones all over the ship and ocean floor attest to the accuracy of the battle reports. Currents from the North Pass feed marine life on the ship and schooling sharks hover around this wreck. It is beautiful but very deep—average depth at about 200ft (61m)—and any dives must be planned well.

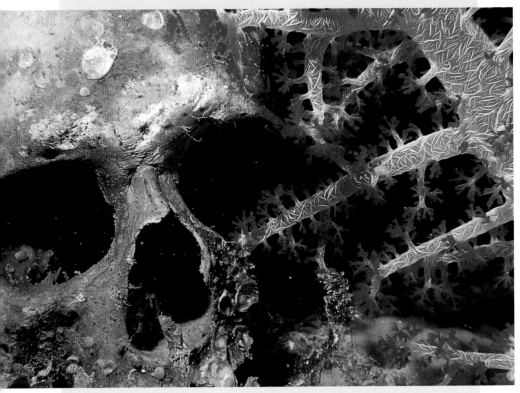

Skulls and bones of Japanese sailors lay scattered around some of the wrecks.

10 *Susuki* Destroyer

This Momi-class destroyer was re-fitted for patrol and was known as Patrol Boat 34 at the time of its sinking. It is normally snorkeled, but it's also a good wreck to penetrate. Inside the four compartments, which can be entered from the deck, are gauges, the ship's wheel, gas masks and other debris. However, two people inside this narrow and silty ship are about as many as can safely penetrate at one time.

The engine room is probably the most interesting. You enter through a narrow

Location: West shore of Tonoas

Depth Range: 10-50ft (3-15m)

Access: Boat/Live-aboard

Expertise Rating: Novice (overswim); Intermediate (for penetration)

but passable skylight. This room houses many gauges, an immense boiler, a generator and various pieces of machinery lay scattered about.

The other rooms are also accessible through skylight entries but always remember that it is very silty. Move sparingly, with careful fin control.

The outside of the ship is also full of surprises, including a large rope sponge formation about midship. Beautiful sponge growth on the bow is accented by white hydroids.

Soft coral grows in the destroyer's window.

A wrasse hides in a rope sponge.

Weno

151°52'30''E

7°25'N

7°

Ette Mokumok

Tonoas

0   .5   1 km
0   .25   .5 miles
not for navigation

Reef
Depth
0-15ft
15-30ft
30-60ft
60-120ft
120ft+

SAPOU

WONPIEPI

Nippo Maru **11**

NECHAP
General's Cave
RORO

7°22'

Hospital Ruins
Shinto Shrine
Catholic Mission

Momokawa Maru **12**
Aikoku Maru

Mt Tonomwan
1128ft

Bombed Fuel Tanks
Dock

San Francisco Maru **14**
Fanamu Island
Kikukawa Maru

NUKUNO   NUKAN
Japanese Seaplane Base
(High School)

17 *Emily Flying Boat & Betty Bomber*

Hoki Maru **16**

Former Airfield
Eten

18 *Fujikawa Maru*

151°52'30''E

Tonoas Dive Sites

	Good Snorkeling	Novice	Intermediate	Advanced
11 *Nippo Maru*				●
12 *Momokawa Maru*			●	
13 *Aikoku Maru*				●
14 *San Francisco Maru*				●
15 *Kikukawa Maru*				●
16 *Hoki Maru*				●
17 Emily Flying Boat & Betty Bomber	●	●		
18 *Fujikawa Maru*	●		●	

11 *Nippo Maru*

After going through the channel and rounding the island tip on the east side of Tonoas, the boat slows as the guide looks for landmarks. The bridge of a medium-sized, upright freighter lies 80ft below. This is one of the best wreck dives in the lagoon.

As you swim down the anchor line, you'll pass bulbous jellyfish that pulse through the nutrient-rich waters. Depending on the day, visibility can reach 100ft, or be as poor as 30ft. On a good day, the ship quickly comes into view. If the current is running, quite a show of marine life—including schools of grey reef sharks and jacks—swims around the bridge area and aft.

The ship's outline shows no sign of damage, but the armaments on deck quickly catch the eye. The *Nippo* was a water carrier, but it also transported wheeled artillery guns and tanks. Near the guns, local guides have positioned a pair

Location: East of Tonoas

Depth Range: 60-145ft+ (18-44m+)

Access: Boat/Live-aboard

Expertise Rating: Advanced

A full medicine chest on the *Nippo Maru*.

The ship's wheel is surrounded by tiny baitfish.

of deer antlers, some cups and some plates—items found inside the ship's galley and various quarters.

The holds provide interesting artifacts. Many sake bottles are intact and the third hold has boxes of ammunition. The aft hold is full of bases for field and shore guns. Objects such as mess kits, boots and gun parts can be seen in the various holds.

Beautiful white gorgonians on the lookout railing at the top of the bridge decorate this ship like a piece of landscaping. The *Nippo*'s bridge can be entered and contains some impressive instruments such as a double-handled telegraph (in the two o'clock position) and compass. The portholes are overgrown for the most part, but the bridge is

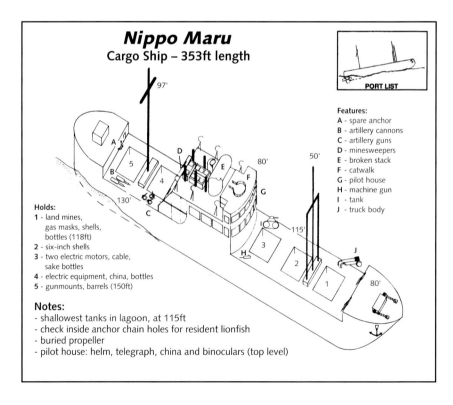

Nippo Maru
Cargo Ship – 353ft length

97'

PORT LIST

Features:
A - spare anchor
B - artillery cannons
C - artillery guns
D - minesweepers
E - broken stack
F - catwalk
G - pilot house
H - machine gun
I - tank
J - truck body

80'
50'
130'
115'
80'

Holds:
1 - land mines, gas masks, shells, bottles (118ft)
2 - six-inch shells
3 - two electric motors, cable, sake bottles
4 - electric equipment, china, bottles
5 - gunmounts, barrels (150ft)

Notes:
- shallowest tanks in lagoon, at 115ft
- check inside anchor chain holes for resident lionfish
- buried propeller
- pilot house: helm, telegraph, china and binoculars (top level)

still quite bright, although a flashlight helps. The ship's wheel is still there, covered with encrusting sponges.

From the bridge, you can descend and follow a passageway that has cabins on both sides. The rear of the midship provides an entrance to the galley, where a multi-plate stove runs the length of the long but narrow room. Pots and pans and other utensils still adorn the walls and stove. It is quite silty, so take care inside.

12 Momokawa Maru

The *Momokawa* is a relatively new find, discovered in 1984. It sits with a heavy list to port, with the bridge and starboard at about 70ft. This ship is not heavily overgrown with marine life, although tubastrea corals adorn the upper kingposts and whip corals appear in patches on the sandy bottom. Bumphead parrotfish schools often graze in the area.

Location: East of Tonoas

Depth Range: 70-130ft (21-40m)

Access: Boat/Live-aboard

Expertise Rating: Intermediate

The three forward holds contain a jumble of airplane parts that were destined to help repair the already crippled Japanese air force. Belly tanks for fighters, engines, wings, fuselage parts and propeller blades are part of the sunken cargo.

Large gun shells and small bombs are also found in the deeper reaches of the forward hold. Portions of trucks also rest in the hold debris. Other artifacts on the ship include a beautiful porcelain serving platter, sake sets and other galley items. A field artillery piece on the stern has some nice coral growth.

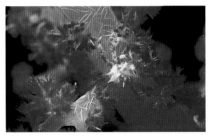

A soft coral crab camouflages to avoid predators.

13 Aikoku Maru

Only the aft half of the *Aikoku Maru* remains, and a portion of that recently collapsed. It sits upright in the lagoon. The ship, from the bow to part of the bridge, was blown apart by the massive explosion that caused her to sink in a matter of seconds.

Location: East of Tonoas

Depth Range: 130-210ft (40-64m)

Access: Boat/Live-aboard

Expertise Rating: Advanced

There are a couple of theories as to how the ship sank. One suggests it was gunned down by attacking U.S. Avengers and that the ship blew up as a result. A third plane flying over during the attack, piloted by a Lt. Briggs and two crew, was apparently destroyed by the blast.

But a Japanese eyewitness says the Avenger was shot down while approaching the ship. The plane crashed into the ship's bridge and fell flaming into the hold. The explosion occurred moments later. One thing is for sure: no one survived this monumental blast.

This ship is deep and unique. The anti-aircraft guns still point to the sky.

The bridge's recent collapse rendered the bridge area and the first two levels impenetrable. But, being a freighter and passenger liner, the ship has many decks that are great to explore. Many men died on this ship and the deep inner recesses are a mass graveyard. Since it is quite deep, follow your guide the first few times around and get to know the wreck before attempting any penetrations.

The skull of a Japanese seaman rests among soft corals.

14 *San Francisco Maru*

The *San Francisco Maru* is one of the best wrecks in Chuuk with well preserved large war relics on its deck and in its holds. Even though it is an old ship, built in 1919, it is deep, which has helped keep it in good shape.

Tanks rest on the main deck at the forward part of the ship—one on the port side and two to starboard. The forward hold contains mines. Old photos show the mines aligned neatly; today, however, there are some gaps in the line-up due to theft—local divers have taken mines to use the powder for dynamite fishing. Although all artifacts are protected on Chuuk, enforcement is difficult.

In the fourth hold, two trucks with their radiators intact have been photographed extensively. The wooden bridge is now all but gone, leaving only the framework. The ship's bell was there until 1978, when it was stolen, again in opposition to Chuukese law.

Location: Southeast of Tonoas

Depth Range: 130-190ft (40-58m)

Access: Boat/Live-aboard

Expertise Rating: Advanced

Tanks sit on the *San Francisco*'s forward deck.

15 *Kikukawa Maru*

Due to an incredible explosion, little remains of the *Kikukawa*. Interestingly, the ship's demise had nothing to do with the American attack.

According to historian Klaus Lindemann, supplies for an outlying garrison in the Marshalls were being loaded on the morning of October 7, 1943, when a fire broke out in the aft hold. Ordnance in the aft holds made the fire a major hazard. Other units dispatched to help the ship's crew fight the blaze, but to no avail. That evening a horrific explosion rocked the islands. Trees on Eten and Tonoas defoliated, windows shattered and some people watching the blaze from shore

Location: Near Fanamu Island

Depth Range: 65-120ft (20-37m)

Access: Boat/Live-aboard

Expertise Rating: Advanced

were killed. The aft and midship were reduced to pieces by the violent explosion. All hands on the ship and the vessels trying to quell the blaze were lost. Today, only the foreship remains.

The name of the ship is still readable on the bow. The force of the explosion is still evident in the buckled plates. This ship is seldom dived and the remains are in extremely good shape, a testament to the idea that low diver-pressure aids shipwreck preservation.

An airplane engine sits in the sand as does part of the engine room. There are propeller blades scattered about. Many anemones adorn this ship and whip corals grow on what's left of the rear of the ship. Amazingly, considering the immense destructive force of the explosion, many plates, cups and intact boxes of food remain in the forward hold.

16 Hoki Maru

The *Hoki* is another one of those ships only partially intact, but what is left is pretty spectacular. The aft hold is literally an undersea parking lot full of trucks, road equipment and other vehicles. Swimming past the hatch-cover frames, you'll see a bulldozer (among other vehicles) resting ominously on the sagging beams. A human bone was placed on one of the truck cabs—presumably the remains of a crewmember found in the

Location: East of Eten

Depth Range: 35-150ft (11-46m)

Access: Boat/Live-aboard

Expertise Rating: Advanced

hold. These trucks are now quite fragile and their chassis, while most intact of any vehicles in the lagoon, are thin from oxidation. Take great care to not touch or bump into these impressive artifacts.

The next hold features an assortment of bombs and mines, bottles and other implements of war and survival.

This is a great wreck for marine life. Look for large schools of batfish around the wreck and cleaning station at the base of the mast, which rises to 30ft. Dogtooth tuna schools also patrol the area, and you'll find cleaning stations near the mast and around what's left of the bridge. Careless divers recently knocked some brilliant red tube sponges from the mast, so be careful when ascending and descending.

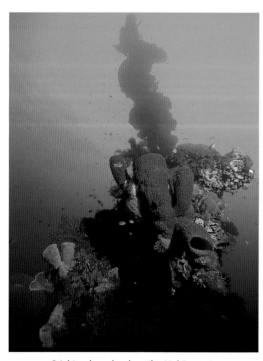

Bright red corals adorn the *Hoki*'s mast.

A diver inspects a human bone left on a truck in this underwater parking lot.

17 Emily Flying Boat & Betty Bomber

Two nice plane wreck dives are fairly close to one another near Eten Island. The large Emily Flying Boat rests near a reef that is rich in marine life, including nudibranchs, crinoids, spawning sea cucumbers and moray eels. The plane itself hosts a good variety of fish, especially small damsels, fusiliers and pygmy sweepers. Some brilliant soft corals adorn the upright pontoon support and sponges encrust the propellers.

Three of the four props are fairly upright, although the plane is pretty much upside-down. The cockpit is penetrable, but the metal is very jagged, so take great care not to get snagged.

This plane was carrying many high-ranking Japanese officers when it was damaged after an incredible encounter

Location: Eten Island Channel

Depth Range: 30-60ft (9-18m)

Access: Boat/Live-aboard

Expertise Rating: Novice

with American planes. There was much gunfire, but the pilot actually hid in a cloud to evade the Americans. The plane was too damaged to land properly, but the pilot managed to get it down safely, and everyone was able to get out before it quickly sank.

The Betty Bomber also struggled to land, but never made it to the runway at Eten, which was, at the time, the major

airstrip. The bomber crashed into the sea just short of the runway. This old plane was stripped of much of its contents and a large door was removed from the side to allow divers to enter. Some items, like the seats and a toilet, sit nearby in the sand. Two coral encrusted engines sit about 40ft away from the main body of the plane. On the undersides of the wings, soft corals and lacey gorgonians make excellent subjects for macrophotography.

The Emily's propellers rest in the sand near Eten.

18 Fujikawa Maru

Location: South of Eten

Depth Range: 30-110ft (9-34m)

Access: Boat/Live-aboard

Expertise Rating: Intermediate

The *Fujikawa* is one of Chuuk's must-dives. It is fairly shallow, has corals, artifacts and easy penetrations. Bow and stern guns grace this 437ft-long cargo ship, which once had passenger accommodations.

The Mitsubishi-built ship took a torpedo hit near Kwajelin earlier in the war and was extensively damaged. It made its way back to Chuuk after a three-day ordeal. During the air strike months later, a single torpedo hit the starboard midships and sank it. Today, divers can enter this gaping hole through the hold behind the bridge.

The *Fuji* sits upright. Its stack starts at 20ft and its rear mast is visible from the surface. The holds are interesting and contain everything from shells, machine guns and airplane wings in the first hold, to an entire Zero fuselage in the second hold. The rear holds aren't as full, but there seems to be more sea life aft.

The bow is loaded with soft corals, sea fans and some sea anemones. Most of these anemones have resident purple anemone shrimp that are great for macrophotography. The anchor chain is massively overgrown and a look up at the bow from the seafloor makes you feel tiny. Jacks often school at the anchor chain and there are lionfish here as well. The mast corals are spectacular. Also look for nudibranchs that can grow quite large.

Passageways are heavily laden with whips and soft corals. An occasional jack or surgeonfish swims through. Thick sponge growth and hard corals have taken over the decks and baitfish hover in swarms near the kingposts. Juvenile schools of barracuda also hover here.

The galley and tiled bathtubs are major attractions. The bow gun's cleaning station is home to a large Napoleon wrasse and schooling blackbar barracuda. Mackerel course the wreck during certain seasons, and guitarfish and other rays can be found in the sand below. This is a great wreck for multiple dives.

Fujikawa Maru
Cargo Ship – 437ft length

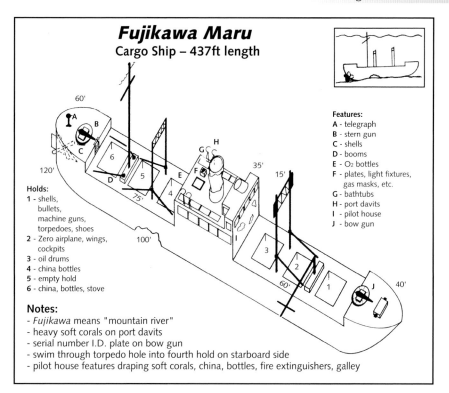

Features:
A - telegraph
B - stern gun
C - shells
D - booms
E - O₂ bottles
F - plates, light fixtures,
    gas masks, etc.
G - bathtubs
H - port davits
I - pilot house
J - bow gun

Holds:
1 - shells,
  bullets,
  machine guns,
  torpedoes, shoes
2 - Zero airplane, wings,
  cockpits
3 - oil drums
4 - china bottles
5 - empty hold
6 - china, bottles, stove

Notes:
- *Fujikawa* means "mountain river"
- heavy soft corals on port davits
- serial number I.D. plate on bow gun
- swim through torpedo hole into fourth hold on starboard side
- pilot house features draping soft corals, china, bottles, fire extinguishers, galley

Lush corals adorn the *Fujikawa's* forward boom.

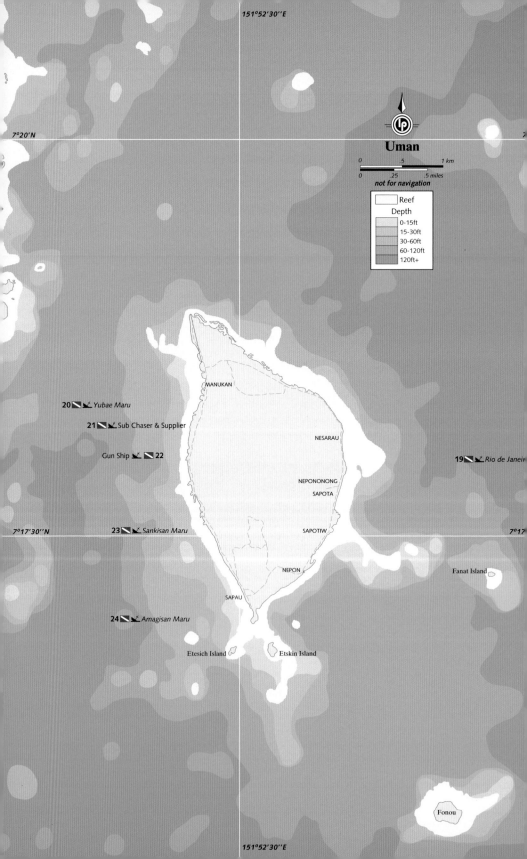

151°52'30''E

7°20'N

Uman

0 .5 1 km

0 .25 .5 miles

not for navigation

Reef

Depth

0-15ft
15-30ft
30-60ft
60-120ft
120ft+

MANUKAN

20 ◤◥⤾ *Yubae Maru*

21 ◤◥⤾ Sub Chaser & Supplier

NESARAU

Gun Ship ⤾◤◥ 22

19 ◤◥⤾ *Rio de Janeir*

NEPONONONG

SAPOTA

7°17'30''N

23 ◤◥⤾ *Sankisan Maru*

SAPOTIW

7°17

NEPON

Fanat Island

SAPAU

24 ◤◥⤾ *Amagisan Maru*

Etesich Island

Etskin Island

Fonou

151°52'30''E

Uman Dive Sites

	Good Snorkeling	Novice	Intermediate	Advanced
19 *Rio de Janeiro Maru*	●		●	
20 *Yubae Maru*			●	
21 Sub Chaser & Supplier	●		●	
22 Gun Ship	●	●		
23 *Sankisan Maru*	●		●	
24 *Amagisan Maru*				●

19 *Rio de Janeiro Maru*

This wreck rests off the southeastern edge of Uman Island in water boasting some of the best visibility in Chuuk Lagoon. Turtles regularly visit the *Rio de Janeiro*, sometimes with remoras swimming along.

The *Rio* was a transport/submarine tender during the war and a passenger vessel before that. Built in 1930, it is the sister ship of the *Heian Maru* and now rests on the bottom on its starboard side at 121ft. The upper portion of the ship sits at about 45ft.

The bridge, along with the rest of the superstructure, is large and dark inside. It is easy to get lost in here. Local guides have brought out items of interest including some beautiful bowls and plates adorned with Japanese designs. Also, look for a pair of bannerfish that lives along the passageway.

Location: Southeast of Uman

Depth Range: 45-121ft (14-37m)

Access: Boat/Live-aboard

Expertise Rating: Intermediate

The *Rio's* exterior is totally overgrown with colorful corals.

The bow gun is still intact and the forward hold contains warheads and immense gun barrels (up to 30ft long) that were probably intended for land field artillery. A big field gun is also buried inside. The stern hold contains cases of old bottles. Be careful, as it is quite silty inside the holds.

Delicate china cups from the ship's cargo.

Many silvery baitfish hang out on the huge stack and in the holds. They seem to move just far enough to keep out of a diver's reach and school tightly when a light or strobe hits them.

Sea whips and soft corals are found aft, where the twin giant propellers make good photographic subjects. Many parts of the stern have nice coral and encrusting invertebrate life.

The rest of the ship is not totally overgrown with coral, but does offer some unique formations. Large platter corals and wire corals grow along the exposed port side and soft corals are present on the bow and in many places on the bridge. Leather and hard coral growth at midship is a haven to a brilliant school of blue damsels.

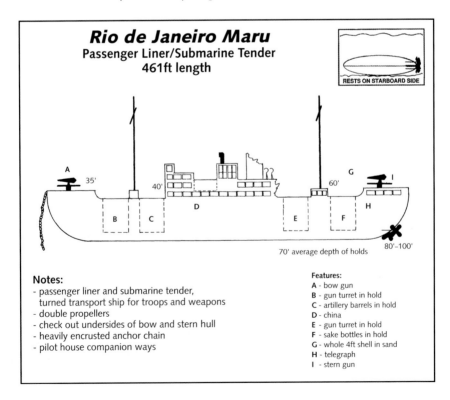

Rio de Janeiro Maru
Passenger Liner/Submarine Tender
461ft length

RESTS ON STARBOARD SIDE

A 35'

40'

G

I

60'

D

H

B   C

E   F

70' average depth of holds

80'-100'

Notes:
- passenger liner and submarine tender, turned transport ship for troops and weapons
- double propellers
- check out undersides of bow and stern hull
- heavily encrusted anchor chain
- pilot house companion ways

Features:
A - bow gun
B - gun turret in hold
C - artillery barrels in hold
D - china
E - gun turret in hold
F - sake bottles in hold
G - whole 4ft shell in sand
H - telegraph
I - stern gun

20 *Yubae Maru*

The *Yubae* was a 305ft coal-burning freighter used by the Japanese Army to transport army supplies. The ship now rests on its side, nearly upside down after having slid down the reef after a storm. The ship is exposed to surge problems after storms and has weakened and collapsed in recent years.

Plates and some cups with insignias rest near the engine room, which is badly mangled and is now a jumble of plates, pipes and fallen catwalks. The bow is

Location: Northwest of Uman

Depth Range: 50-115ft (15-35m)

Access: Boat/Live-aboard

Expertise Rating: Intermediate

overgrown with coral sea whips, soft corals and neon corals, along with a few coral fans.

Remnants of the *Yubae* include a porthole and piles of jumbled wreckage.

21 Sub Chaser & Supplier

Location: West of Uman

Depth Range: 40-85ft (12-26m)

Access: Boat/Live-aboard

Expertise Rating: Intermediate

Two small wrecks rest quite close to the popular *Sankisan Maru* but have been largely ignored over the years. They are small, but great for those who want to see nice coral growth and sessile marine life.

The shallower wreck, an upside-down sub chaser, landed with a slight list. It sits in a reef area with lots of good coral growth. A strange bulge sticking out from the hull is probably a detection device enabling the chaser to communicate with the sub. About midship, a large, passable opening allows you to explore the insides. Lots of glassy sweepers live in here, as well as bigeyes and some angelfish. Divers carrying flashlights can poke into the dark engine room. Beware of the oil that is trapped in the upper reaches of the hull.

Nearby, at 60ft, rests an inter-island supply vessel that has become a beautiful mini-reef. This 120ft-long ship has an aft propeller and rudder area covered in corals. The bow is a true garden and the entire ship supports all sorts of fish life. The small bridge is full of sweepers and the engine room skylights are encrusted but still show intact glass. For the skinny and adventurous, the engine room can be entered without much difficulty.

This wreck never used to be visited at all, and there is now evidence of recent diver wear and tear. Realize the marine growth on this ship is special and dive here with extreme care. Photographers will have lots of fun on this little ship.

22 Gun Ship

A diver explores the photogenic bow gun.

Location: West of Uman

Depth Range: 3-70ft (1-21m)

Access: Boat/Live-aboard

Expertise Rating: Novice

This wreck may be Chuuk's most recognizable icon. With its bow gun sitting in about 3ft at low tide, the ship, known as the *Hino Maru 2*, is an underwater photography studio.

Shooting with a downward camera angle can make the wreck appear much deeper than it actually is. If you shoot at eye-level, or with an upward camera angle, your model's reflection against the shimmering surface will also make a striking image. Take a shot or two of the resident damselfish that lives in the barrel of the gun. The gun has sagged downward in recent years, but is still good for snorkeling.

Other than a winch below the gun, which is overgrown with coral but still distinguishable, there isn't much left on deck. Inside the ship, the sun shines through a series of posts, causing shafts of light and shadows to form an ominous cathedral effect.

Soft corals, which make excellent macrophotography subjects, adorn the inside of the wreck, and some whips and fans grow along the outer sides. The rest of the ship was blown to bits—its mangeled parts can be seen strewn all over the seafloor.

The *Hino Maru 2* gun ship's shallow bow is covered with corals and is excellent for snorkeling.

23 *Sankisan Maru*

This ship has great upper marine growth on the mast and on the cargo booms and is excellent for snorkeling and snorkeling photos. Some growth has been knocked off by poor anchoring practices in recent years, but there are still lots of macro subjects in shallow water.

Location: Southwest of Uman

Depth Range: 2-90ft (1-27m)

Access: Boat/Live-aboard

Expertise Rating: Intermediate

Launched from Harima Dockyard on January 29, 1942, the *Sankisan* had a very short career in both civilian and military service. It went down after suffering a hit that caused a devastating explosion—the hit apparently struck the aft hold, which was full of ordnance. Amazingly, the rest of the wreck is in surprisingly good shape.

The ship was a medium-sized freighter that now rests upright on a slope, southwest of Uman. The foremast breaks the surface and the coral-laden crosstree is at only 10ft. What's left of the stern is much deeper—far past the blast crater—at about 150ft. Most of the diving on the *Sankisan* is in the 50 to 80ft range, the average depth inside the holds.

The cargo of the *Sankisan* comes into view as you descend to the deck, where you'll see the truck chassis—tires on wheels, engine, radiator, drive train

and steering wheel. The first hold still stores scores of bullets. The ammunition was in boxes, but fierce typhoon waves shook the ship a few years ago, collapsing the fragile wooden boxes and damaging some of the coral and structures around the bow deck. The

Bullets found on the *Sankisan*.

The shallow mast provides great snorkeling.

bullets now lie in heaps, boxes and spread out in clips.

Divers get tempted to slip a souvenir bullet or two into their BCs, but remember, it is against the law to remove anything from the wrecks and Chuuk levies a stiff fine. Guides occasionally check divers for infractions. Also, this ammunition is very unstable after years of submersion—it is dangerous to handle and should only be observed. The detonators are particularly dangerous and should not be messed with.

The next hold has an upright truck with tires, steering wheel and radiator still in place although the body has rusted off. The hold after that has a

Coral formations now cover the ship's davits.

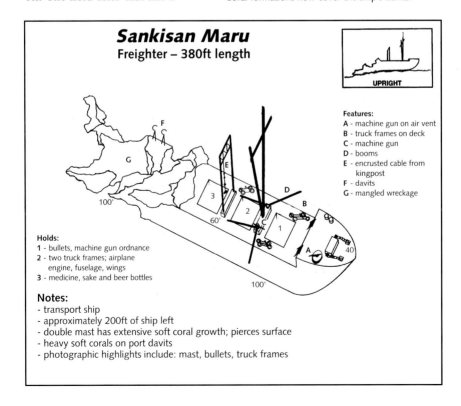

Sankisan Maru
Freighter – 380ft length

UPRIGHT

Features:
A - machine gun on air vent
B - truck frames on deck
C - machine gun
D - booms
E - encrusted cable from kingpost
F - davits
G - mangled wreckage

Holds:
1 - bullets, machine gun ordnance
2 - two truck frames; airplane engine, fuselage, wings
3 - medicine, sake and beer bottles

Notes:
- transport ship
- approximately 200ft of ship left
- double mast has extensive soft coral growth; pierces surface
- heavy soft corals on port davits
- photographic highlights include: mast, bullets, truck frames

nice assortment of small bottles in many sizes and colors.

Plating near the bow shows the incredible force of the explosion that destroyed the stern. It is wavy and rippled like a potato chip. On the outer hull you'll find some delicate brittle stars on an encrusting sponge—great for macrophotography. Sea cucumbers graze on calcareous algae. The anchor chain is also a garden of encrusting marine life.

The *Sankisan* ranks as one of the prettiest wrecks on Chuuk, with coral growth all over the deck (copper ions released from the ammo prevent growth in the holds). The foremast and the kingpost top at 10ft host a variety of creatures, making this a superb safety decompression stop.

24 *Amagisan Maru*

Sitting in the channel off the southwest tip of Uman Island is a ship not many people dive, despite its nice war relics. The *Amagisan Maru* obviously took a big hit, which becomes apparent as you descend into the clear water. Resting at a 46° angle on its port side, the ship is pretty clean and its outline unfettered by abundant marine growth.

It'll take a couple of dives to explore this ship, as it is a very large freighter and one of the deeper lagoon wrecks. The stern is at about 190ft, the bow is at about

Location: Southwest of Uman Island

Depth Range: 100-190ft (31-60m)

Access: Boat/Live-aboard

Expertise Rating: Advanced

100ft and the bridge area is at about 120ft. The huge torpedo hole to starboard, with a large and long display of sea whips covering its perimeter, is large enough for two divers to easily swim through.

The niftiest item is a car sitting on the bottom of the second hold. It must have tumbled during the sinking, as the body and the chassis don't properly align. This fancy vehicle, a large sedan, was probably being delivered to a high-ranking officer. Above the car, some enlisted men's transportation—bicycles—are encrusted but in good shape. In the shallowest forward hold a tank truck sits at 135ft.

The aft requires a planned decompression dive to properly see it all. It has a rear gun mounted on the platform. If the water is clear, a shallower over-swim reveals these features.

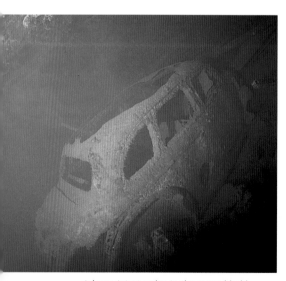

A large, intact sedan in the second hold.

Chuuk Lagoon Reefs

Chuuk is known for its wrecks, but more and more exploration is being done on the reefs and with excellent results. The passes, or wide channels, that cut the atoll's outer barrier reef and allow ships to come and go, are bottlenecks or funnels for water coming into the lagoon. The rushing, current-fed waters pass by the channel edges whose dramatic drop-offs teem with fish life.

Drift diving is normally done along the outer walls and in the passes. There are also good islands for picnicking and shallow reef areas that make for excellent snorkeling.

The outer barrier reef feeds the North Pass with pelagic marine life.

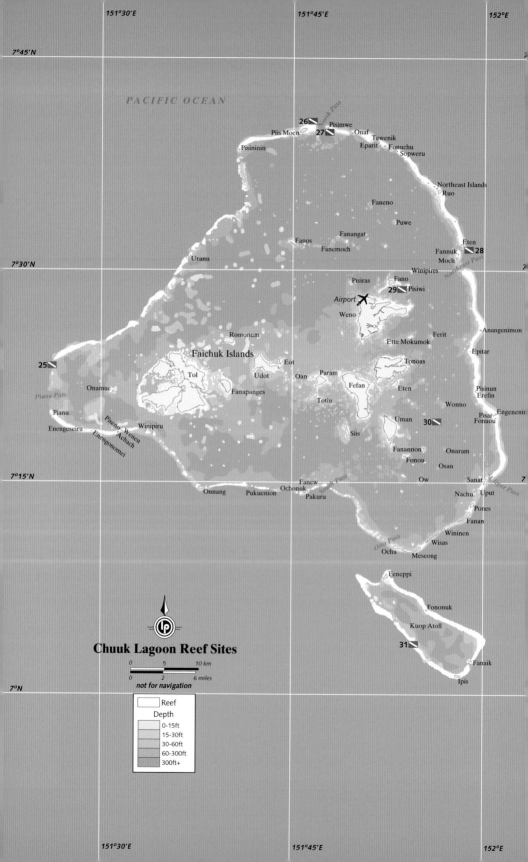

PACIFIC OCEAN

26 Piis Moen Pisimwe
27 Onaf
Tewenik
Eparit Fonuchu
Sopweru

Pisininin

Northeast Islands
Ruo

Faneno
Puwe

Fanos Fanangat
Fanemoch

Uranu

Eten
Fannuk 28
Moch

Winipires
Pisiras Fano
29 Pisiwi

Airport
Weno

Romonum
Ferit
Ette Mokumok

Faichuk Islands

Eot
Udot Oan Param Tonoas
Fanapanges Totiu Fefan Eten

Tol

Onamue Siis Wonno

Pianu Winipiru Uman 30
Enengeseiru Enengonomei Piseno Wenen Achach Fanannon Onaram
Fonou Osan

Fanew Ow Sanat
Onnang Pukuenion Ochonuk Nachu Uput
Pakuru Pones

Anangenimon

Epitar

Pisinun
Erefin
Pisar Engenenir
Fonuoui

Fanan
Wininen
Wisas
Ocha Meseong

Feneppi

Fononuk

Kuop Atoll

31

Fanaik

Ipis

Chuuk Lagoon Reef Sites

0   5   10 km
0   2   6 miles
not for navigation

Reef
Depth
0-15ft
15-30ft
30-60ft
60-300ft
300ft+

Chuuk Lagoon - Reefs Dive Sites

	Good Snorkeling	Novice	Intermediate	Advanced
25 Cannon Island Drop-Off	●		●	
26 North Pass	●		●	
27 Pisimwe Island	●	●		
28 Northeast Pass	●		●	
29 Pisiwi Island	●	●		
30 Jeep Island	●	●		
31 Kuop Atoll	●		●	

25 Cannon Island Drop-Off

West of Tol, a small island in the Northwest Pass called Uranu still displays Japanese armaments ready to defend the pass. All of the pass islands used to have big shore guns, but this is one of only two islands left that still has them. Along the outer reef the boat stops at a double reef where divers enter the water and head for the pass mouth. The sheer wall provides lots of drift- and wall-diving action.

The coral growth is attractive, especially below 25 to 30ft on the sharply sloping reef. The reef follows the sloping contour and schools of yellowtail fusiliers run up and down it. Fish such as bigeyes, groupers and even an occasional turtle entice divers. Territorial grey reefs, silvertips and shyer whitetip reef sharks are present, especially when fishermen come to the island to fish and camp.

The wall comes to a corner and falls off straight down, with some slight down currents, and there is a

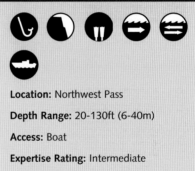

Location: Northwest Pass

Depth Range: 20-130ft (6-40m)

Access: Boat

Expertise Rating: Intermediate

Yellowtail fusiliers are common on the outer reefs.

profusion of sea fans, fish and sharks. In this true abyss, the sharks approach nose to mask before veering away. As this is a prime fishing spot, they are accustomed to vying for a meal with fishermen and often come to check out the divers. The reef gains more contour again, but the sharks remain either territorial, curious or hopeful of stealing a spearfished meal as they streak by over the reef.

At the channel, you have the option of going across or swimming up the channel walls. The coral has interesting formations and is good for decompression after the deep wall dive. Check out the big platter corals in this area.

After the dive, go visit the island for lunch. Turtle fishermen sometimes use it during turtle season (Chuuk has a legal sea turtle hunting season), but it is normally uninhabited. You can walk around the entire island in about five minutes. Snorkeling is pleasant here at high tide.

A sea fan adorns the deep wall at Cannon Island.

Turtle Hunting

Remains of a hunted turtle in Chuuk Lagoon.

Sea turtle hunting is legal in Chuuk State, although hunting season varies from year to year. Sea turtles are considered a staple in the local diet, and have long been a traditional source of protein. Hunters are supposed to take only what they need to feed their families, but many hunt for their entire village and may take more than one. The shells of the hawksbill turtles are used to make jewelry, some of which you may see for sale in handicraft stores. As no conservation officers monitor this practice, it is hard to discern the impact turtle trade has on sea turtle populations, as the size and sex of the turtles is not currently recorded. Remember that sea turtles are endangered species. Help protect the depleted populations by not buying goods—be it turtle soup or turtle shell jewelry—that encourage turtle hunting.

26 North Pass

This dive starts outside the pass at a large pinnacle that rises to within 10ft of the surface. The water here is extremely clear, even at low tide. You swim to the west along the outer reef wall, which slopes gradually. You then drift dive going out with the current into the pass.

Location: West side of North Pass

Depth Range: 10-130ft (3-40m)

Access: Boat

Expertise Rating: Intermediate

This is a relaxed dive with some coral growth. Hard corals dominate, including large star and brain corals. Crinoids reach out from outcrops. Because this is an outer reef, bigger fish such as bumphead parrotfish cruise the deeper reaches and schools of tuna come in quite close, showing flashes of silver and high-speed swimming action.

The clear water lets you see lots of medium-sized tridacna clams at 20 to 30ft. At this depth, some shallow coral canyons are worth exploring. Returning through the pass is also exciting because you drift into the lagoon with the tide. The chances of seeing big sharks and pelagic fish here are very good. More than once, on calm days, a school of spinner dolphins has joined the boat on the way back from the pass. They are incredible acrobats that jump, spin and flip out of the water.

Tridacna clams appear in many colors.

27 Pisimwe Island

This island is a must-stop after a dive in the North Pass. It is essentially just a sand spit surrounded by big stands of staghorn coral that are most easily snorkeled at high tide. It has coconut trees and white, sandy beaches and is a haven for all kinds of birds including cranes, boobies, terns and Pacific white birds. Watch your step, as some birds lay eggs on top of the beach's white gravelly sand. They will probably buzz you if you get too close.

Location: North Pass

Depth Range: 10-8ft (3-2.5m)

Access: Boat

Expertise Rating: Novice

Get a picture of yourself on this Robinson Crusoe isle. It is a true tropical paradise on a tiny spit of sand.

This island is much cleaner than most accessible islands in Chuuk, so be sure to pack out what you bring in and take some extra litter if you can, to help keep this island in its marvelously pristine state.

Idyllic Pisimwe Island makes an excellent retreat for lunch or a decompression stop between dives.

28 Northeast Pass

This is a great place to see some truly idyllic islands. There are three small, coconut-tree-covered islets near the cuts here. Their tranquility, as the sky reflects off the water with the lagoon

Location: Outer reef, northeast cut

Depth Range: 30-130ft (9-40m)

Access: Boat

Expertise Rating: Intermediate

Lively purple basslets teem around the corals.

islands in the background, makes it hard to believe a major air battle took place here.

Visibility is excellent—so gin-clear that you must monitor your depth to make sure you're not blowing your dive profile by going too deep.

Underwater rolling hills rise to 30 or 40ft then fall off into 70-to-80ft-deep valleys. Out toward the open sea, the bottom gradually slopes to beyond 130ft. You will find many hard corals and platter corals with small crinoids stretching out in the daytime. Coral coverage gets better as you swim north, where the reef is thick with staghorn patches and clouds of silver chromis.

Large, delicate platter corals provide coverage for bigeyes and soldierfish. Blue-stripe fusiliers swarm over this coral, circling divers in a swirl of color. This is a great place to find a clear spot, relax, and watch all the action in a beautiful, real-life aquarium. Manta rays are occasionally seen farther up the channel.

29 Pisiwi Island

This is a picnic island where visitors sit on the beach and enjoy the ambiance of a tropical lagoon. During the week, it is virtually empty, although it is a favorite local hangout on weekends. There may be a charge for a daytrip here, depending on the mood of the operator.

This is a shallow site—30ft is about the deepest you'll go. Just below the surface, you'll find patch reefs and big stands of staghorn coral with juveniles and blue chromis hiding within the branches.

The north end of the island is for more adventurous snorkelers. It is only a few feet deep but leads to a small outer

Location: Inner Lagoon, near Weno

Depth Range: 2-30ft (1-9m)

Access: Boat

Expertise Rating: Novice

breakwater reef where blacktip reef sharks are frequent visitors. Look to the shallow areas for a fin coursing back and forth by the nearby patch reef. That fin might belong to an eagle ray—also a frequent visitor to this site.

Photographing an anemone at Pisiwi Island.

30   Jeep Island

Like Pisimwe, this island has just a smattering of palms and some shell- and sand-covered shores. The difference is that Jeep is set up for daytrips, snorkeling excursions, overnight and week-long trips. The island is owned by the Blue Lagoon Resort, which services the island with meals, diving and boat trips. A Chuukese couple on the island caters to guests. As many as 12 people can spend a week at this tiny outpost, exploring surrounding wrecks and reefs. It has a small but sturdy bungalow and an outdoor eating area. People sleep inside on comfy futons or under the stars if the weather permits.

The nearby reefs are part of a saddle system that dips down and then comes up to form a tiny island chain inside the

Location: Northeast of Uman

Depth Range: 9-65ft (3-20m)

Access: Boat/Beach

Expertise Rating: Novice

lagoon. The reef diving can be good, with silvertip sharks coming in to see what's happening, lots of staghorn and other hard coral formations. Lovers of small invertebrates will enjoy these environs.

For those not wanting to go too far from the beachside lounge chairs, the snorkeling is quite nice, especially on the lagoon side of the tiny island.

Jeep Island provides a unique, rustic retreat.

31 Kuop Atoll

Due to its remoteness, this uninhabited atoll is rarely dived, although it is quite accessible when the seas are calm. Unlike the lagoon, the water around the outer reef of Kuop is gin clear. Hard corals are healthy and varied, with lots of nice stands of lettuce corals and plenty of small tropicals and bluestripe fusiliers.

Location: South of South & Otta Passes

Depth Range: 8-130ft+ (2-40m+)

Access: Boat/Live-aboard

Expertise Rating: Intermediate

It is also a good place to see sea turtles. The reef plunges into an incredible bottomless abyss along a steep, short slope and the possibility of seeing good pelagic life along the outer reaches is excellent.

Kuop's southern tip has been touted as one of the world's greatest dives and, while that may be a bit generous, it is full of action. Along a series of sandy channels leading to a wall, you can see such pelagics as blackbar barracuda, grey and whitetip sharks. Also look for eagle rays hiding in the sand. At around 90ft, hang out at the current-swept

Thick leather corals bloom along the Kuop Atoll reef.

tip and watch the fish and sharks go by. In the shallows, the current disappears and you can enjoy lots of macro critters.

Research by historian Klaus Lindemann shows that the *Tachikaze* destroyer was hit near Kuop and beached itself on the reef. Searches for the ship have come up empty; to date, no remains have been found. It is believed that the stricken ship probably sank along the southwest shore and eventually slipped off the reef and into the depths. Any telltale signs may be overgrown by now, but for those wanting to find a new wreck, the final resting place of the *Tachikaze* still remains a mystery.

Chuuk's Outer Islands

Life on Chuuk's outer islands remains much the same as it has for centuries. These atolls are home to star-navigators, people who can ply the open seas in large, hand-hewn, sail-powered canoes using only the stars and the waves as their guides. Sustained by the sea and the land, the people exist on a diet of fish, taro, banana, breadfruit, sweet potato and some intrusion of rice.

A trip to the outer islands is sure to be a memorable experience but the logistics are complicated and arrangements should be made at least several months in advance.

The SS *Thorfinn* makes trips to the atolls between Chuuk and Yap in June and July. These expeditions include diving, sailing on traditional canoes and island and village visits. Welcoming dances are often performed by the locals and these lively and colorful events are not to be missed.

The diving out here can be high-voltage, with swirling packs of silvertip sharks, an occasional oceanic whitetip and big schools of fish. Colorful invertebrate life tends to be deep in the extremely clear water; visibility averages 150ft (46m). Much of the diving is still exploratory. Starting at 100ft (30m) and running along sloping walls on most of the atolls, fields of golden sea fans, crimson sea whips and giant soft corals grow in abundance.

This is also prime sea turtle-viewing country. Many of the atolls are uninhabited and set aside as "garden islands" by tradition. Mating green sea turtles are common. Many of the turtles still grow large to a mature age at these natural conservation sites. Tabu—a restriction giving only those who "garden" an atoll permission to use its resources—allows only certain people to fish and hunt turtles.

There are no facilities for visitors on the outer islands and the residents live a very traditional lifestyle. Their language and customs vary greatly from those of the people in the Chuuk Lagoon.

Outer Islanders traditionally use the stars and sun to navigate canoes.

Pohnpei is the quintessential picture of tropical splendor. Rugged, jungled and razorbacked, it reigns as the highest island in the FSM. Its peaks get plenty of annual rainfall, which feeds more than 40 rivers that nourish the lush upper rainforest.

Pohnpei's waterfalls range from pleasant to spectacular and visiting them is a refreshing and breathtaking experience for anyone venturing to the base of the falls. You can even camp at some sites and listen to the tumble of falling water as you sleep under the tropical sky. The streams are great for cooling off after a hike in the hills.

Pohnpei's people offer a look at family life island-style. Communities come together to weave a new boat house or just to wash the daily laundry. Children frolic in the many rivers that flow from the mountains and down past the villages.

Although local tourism offices now embrace diving as a means to attract tourists, in the past Pohnpei dive operations were pretty much on their own. Low diver-impact and small groups make the diving experience much different than at busier Pacific resorts.

Diving amenities here are quite basic—nothing too fancy except the brilliant underwater scenery. Tanks, weights and some rental gear is available. Currently no live-aboards service the area. Fiberglass dive boats with medium-sized outboards are the norm. This is actually part of the charm and adventure of diving here.

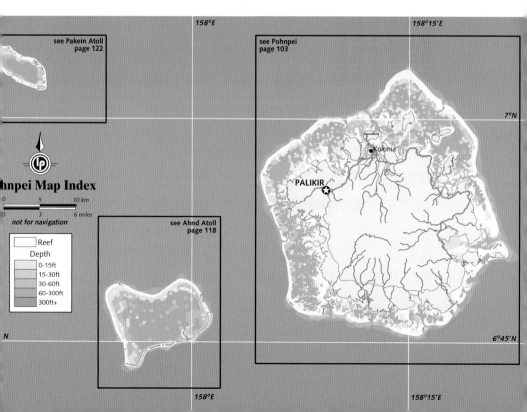

see Pakein Atoll
page 122

see Pohnpei
page 103

see Ahnd Atoll
page 118

158°E

158°15'E

7°N

6°45'N

158°E

158°15'E

Kolonia

PALIKIR

hnpei Map Index

0   5   10 km

0   3   6 miles

not for navigation

Reef

Depth

0-15ft
15-30ft
30-60ft
60-300ft
300ft+

N

Snorkelers can explore shallow inner lagoon walls that are covered in corals.

Pohnpei Dive Sites

	Good Snorkeling	Novice	Intermediate	Advanced
32 Mwand Wall & Pass	●		●	
33 Manta Road	●		●	
34 Areu Wall	●		●	
35 Na Island	●		●	
36 Lost City (Nan Madol)	●		●	
37 Joy Island	●		●	
38 Ros & Nahtik Islands			●	
39 Nahlap Island (Rainbow Island)			●	
40 Kehpara Island (Black Coral Island)	●		●	
41 Poahloang Pass	●		●	
42 Poahloang Mouth				●
43 Dawahk Pass	●			●
44 Inner Sanctum	●	●		
45 Palikir Pass	●		●	
46 Palikir Wall	●		●	

Pohnpei

32 Mwand Wall & Pass

This is a beautiful dive site with long, branching growths of evergreen tubastrea corals, fields of red whip corals, and soft tree corals in magnificent hues of yellow, burnt orange and burgundy. The reef starts within 5 to 10ft of the surface and quickly slopes down.

The prettiest parts of the reef decorated with the most sea life are found in 40 to 80ft. Napoleon wrasse patrol the deeper water and schools of fusiliers cruise along the reef line.

This is also a good site for macro critters. Crinoids in many sizes and colors, feather stars, various nudibranchs and a host of blennies, anthias and chromis appear in the shallower reaches.

Below 100ft, big branching gorgonian sea fans join a few black-coral trees along

Location: Mwand Pass, northeast Pohnpei

Depth Range: 10-100ft (3-30m)

Access: Boat

Expertise Rating: Intermediate

the ledges. The currents change here frequently so you may wind up swimming toward the mouth of the pass at the start of the dive, only to find yourself drifting back to shallower water halfway through the dive.

The variety of wide-angle and close-up possibilities brings photographers back for multiple dives. Biologists will also find good macro creatures to study.

Crimson sea whips stretch out into the current along Mwand Wall.

33 Manta Road

Many Micronesian islands have a site for spotting manta rays. Manta Road is Pohnpei's manta hotspot. A current of some sort will likely be running here, so check the tide tables to decide what kind of manta behavior you want to observe. At lesser tide movement, mantas take the time to visit cleaning stations, cavort and mate (from January to April). As the water movement increases, feeding and cruising become more of a priority.

Location: Mwand Pass, northeast Pohnpei

Depth Range: 10-80ft (3-24m)

Access: Boat

Expertise Rating: Intermediate

The channel has some nice sandy areas with small cleaning stations and one huge bommie. Farther up the channel another bommie provides a rest stop for whitetip sharks and triggerfish. Avoid toothy triggerfish if they are nesting, as they've been known to chase and nip divers.

Patience is the key to seeing mantas as they move up and down the channels. They habitually pass by the cleaning areas, so find a good spot and gently settle down. Avoid grabbing the coral.

If they aren't chased or feeling threatened, mantas are curious and will approach divers quite closely. Do not attempt to touch or swim after the rays. This upsets their routine and they will leave and not return. Keep your bubbles to a minimum by exhaling gently and slowly.

The color variety of mantas at Manta Road can be quite good as well. They range from almost jet black to light grey with a bright, white belly. Look for remoras using their siphon-like dorsal fins to hitchhike a ride on the rays. The remoras are a good indication that the rays probably leave the channel and forage for plankton in the open sea. Many rays are observed with pilotfish swimming near their mouths. These tiny, yellow-striped jacks use their host as protection, like a kind of moving coral head.

Given the right set of circumstances, a dive at Manta Road can be a mystical and unforgettable experience. In some places mantas have been observed leaping completely out of the water, smashing back down with a big splash.

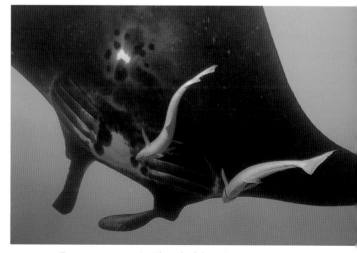

Two remoras cavort with a playful manta ray.

Photographing Mantas

Some of the same problems with shipwreck photography arise photographing manta rays. Mantas reside in channels because the waters are rich in nutrients. Just as silt causes backscatter problems on shipwrecks, the planktonic matter in channels is also highly reflective.

The second problem involves color. Mantas' backs are normally dark gray to black, while their undersides are white. To capture their natural color without making their bellies shine like the moon and their surroundings look like stars in the sky, you'll want to power down.

Shooting with your strobe at one-half power or even one-quarter power is helpful in reducing the scatter problem, filling in the white belly to give a natural appearance. Reduced power also takes the strobe less time to recycle, which is important as the mantas do come close, but they don't always stick around.

Stay put and breathe easy. You can virtually kiss your manta shooting goodbye if you start chasing them. They are curious and will come your way sooner or later.

Lens choice is really up to you. If you want to get some of the reef's corals or fish life in the foreground and keep the mantas in the mid-ground, use your wide-angle; 20mm to 50mm is an acceptable lens range. Film choice again depends on the effect you want to create, but 100 ASA will give you needed depth of field and shutter speed, while keeping the grain down.

For video, remember the picture is supposed to be moving, not the camera. Let the animals swim to the camera and in and out of frame. If you must move the camera, remember to pan with the action. In other words, follow the animal. Don't even touch the zoom button. Underwater zooms are rarely effective.

34　Areu Wall

This inner-lagoon dive is on the eastern side of Pohnpei, north of Areu Point. The reef life is an excellent mix of invertebrates, small fish, large corals and sea fans. The encrusting sponges, tunicates and ascidian colonies make colorful undersea bouquets and the nutrient-swept walls feature black coral, some very large gorgonians and lots of soft coral trees in many hues and shapes. Large wire corals are also found growing along the wall, along with small fields of bright red sea whips.

Location: Near Uh Pass

Depth Range: 5-110ft (2-34m)

Access: Boat

Expertise Rating: Intermediate

Larger reef life is not as abundant, but mantas sometimes swim along the wall as Manta Road is not too far away. Schooling blackbar barracuda and white-tip reef sharks also visit the wall.

This site is great for macrophotographers. Look for sharpnose hawkfish on sea fans, a variety of nudibranchs and flatworms, clownfish and anemones and, at night, soft coral crabs. You can go deep, but for a nice long drift the best parts are in 20 to 60ft. At Areu Point, look for the wall of golden sea fans running along the reef face.

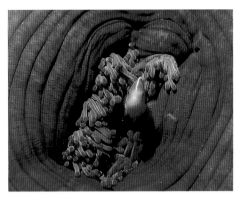

A skunk clownfish peers out from an anemone.

35　Na Island

This is an idyllic island stopover for people visiting the Nan Madol ruins. The beach is covered with white sand, palms and logs that make good resting benches. Often guides wait here until the tide rises, so visitors have time to walk around, eat lunch and explore this uninhabited island. It is also a good place to snorkel and cool off while waiting for the tide.

In the shallows you'll find elkhorn corals, large forests of staghorn coral with tons of chromis and other small tropicals, soft corals and white, sandy canyons in between the coral heads.

Location: East of Temwen Island

Depth Range: 6-95ft (2-29m)

Access: Boat

Expertise Rating: Intermediate

Deeper down are big plate corals and mushroom formations. The hard coral forests are worth a good look as they are home to many different kinds of juvenile fish. Look for the tiny yellow-spotted box puffers.

Colorful schools of basslets dash in and out of staghorn corals.

STEFANIE BRENDL

36 Lost City (Nan Madol)

The outer wall of the Nan Madol ruins (near Nan Dowas) abuts the sea and a diver can have a fascinating archeological dive. As it is so close to the mangroves, don't expect great visibility, and if the wind is blowing in from the east, forget it. But on calm days, this can be a very unique log entry.

The main part of this dive is between 60 and 70ft, where many of the coral-covered basalt pillars now rest in a jumbled heap on the sea floor. Some point upward while others lie down—it is quite a spectacle. Please remember that Nan Madol is a sacred, magical site for Pohnpeians, so act respectfully on the boat, while exploring the ancient ruins, and diving or snorkeling.

Location: East Temwen Island

Depth Range: 10-70ft (3-21m)

Access: Boat

Expertise Rating: Intermediate

The zone between the sea and the mangroves is home to unique crabs, pipefish, hydroids and anemones. Hard corals cover the basalt logs.

Despite the sometimes bad visibility, this can be a good spot for macrophotographers. The anemones host shrimp and the good coral variety supports diverse fish life.

A snorkeler pursues a hermit crab that moves through the channels around Nan Madol.

37 Joy Island

The popular sites around this island are found on the east and northeast shores, but good spots occur all along this stretch of reef. Longtime Pohnpeian divers talk about the light diffusion in the water here, saying if done at the right time of day, the dive can be truly mystical.

Location: Eastern fringing reef

Depth Range: 3-120ft (1-37m)

Access: Boat/Beach

Expertise Rating: Intermediate

Green sea turtles are frequently observed in the area. Reef sharks like to patrol the reef and since the current here can be swift, dogtooth tuna and barracuda schools swoop in with the tide movement.

This site is often used for multiple dives, and a rest on Joy Island is usually part of the day. Take the time to snorkel around the island, especially on the north end and in the access channel. Look for rays in these waters as well.

Prowling blackbar barracuda move with the tide.

38 Ros & Nahtik Islands

These islands on the southern barrier reef are Pohnpei's fastest-disappearing islands due to natural erosion and storms. Between them runs a channel where mantas and lots of other sea life gather. Dives can be done in the channel, at its mouth, or along the outer reef walls. The channel dives can be a little tougher due to currents.

Location: Southern barrier reef

Depth Range: 15-130ft (5-40m)

Access: Boat

Expertise Rating: Intermediate

The outside barrier reef boasts vertical walls along the eastern and southern shores of Ros Island. Expect to see green sea turtles. Lots of schooling reef fish like snapper and jacks visit the water column. Keep an eye out for prowling fish that look like floating logs in the distance. Once you get closer, you realize the "logs" are barracuda—big, fierce-looking fish that are normally harmless and curious—just don't wear anything shiny, as shiny objects are thought to

Wendolin Lionis shows off a trumpet shell found in shallow water.

attract them. Reef sharks are also common here.

Take time to explore the surge channels, grottoes and small caves formed by the surf and eastern trade winds. Look for shells and nudibranchs, including small cowries, large Triton's trumpets and small tridacna clams. Sea pens are among the unusual invertebrates that can be observed on the sea floor.

39 Nahlap Island (Rainbow Island)

Location: Southern barrier reef

Depth Range: 30-130ft (9-40m)

Access: Boat

Expertise Rating: Intermediate

This is another southern island that adjoins a channel, but most of the diving is done on the outside barrier reef. This area has walls and slopes that feature a nice variety of soft corals, good hard corals and sponge life. Many varieties of sea anemones are also found here.

This can be a good place to see pelagic life, such as big king mackerel, jacks, rainbow runners, sharks, turtles and schools of unicornfish and surgeonfish.

Also look for roaming schools of parrotfish along the upper reef.

For fish people, this place can be a bonanza. Coral trout and marbled groupers join a variety of butterflyfish, regal and blue-face angelfish, and thick groups of damsels. This site also has small caverns and overhangs from the wave and current action. Divers can dip down quite deep here, but there's also a lot to see in the 60 to 80ft range.

Schooling jacks patrol the island waters.

40 Kehpara Island (Black Coral Island)

This island is home to the small Black Coral Resort and is sometimes referred to as Black Coral Island. The dives are mostly on the outer barrier wall and reef and can be really exciting dives.

Large Napoleon wrasse are common in these waters as are reef sharks and jacks. Look for schooling tuna and barracuda when the current is working in the channel. A drift dive through the channel is exhilarating although surge can be a problem if there are swells outside the barrier reef.

The wall is a real beauty, decorated with golden sea fans, sponge formations, a good variety of sea anemones and other invertebrate life, including soft corals. Pelagics include beautiful and powerful silvertip, blacktip and whitetip reef sharks.

Macrophotographers like this spot as the shallow portions produce some interesting critters such as nudibranchs, flatworms and a variety of sponge formations. Lobsters also seem to like it here. Where there are

Location: Southwest barrier reef

Depth Range: 20-120ft (6-37m)

Access: Boat

Expertise Rating: Intermediate

lobsters there are usually shells, so look for cowries, spider conchs, tridacna clams, whelks, top shells and cone shells in the sand—especially at night.

Look for large Napolean wrasse.

41 Poahloang Pass

While the pass is usually dived in conjunction with a visit to the mouth, it should be considered a dive in and of itself. The sloping inner reef is full of healthy corals and cracks and crevices. The upper reef stretches endlessly and is home to schooling fish like yellow and black sweetlips, grey snapper and yellow-striped snapper.

Sea turtles rest on the coral ledges and you can approach closely if you

Location: Poahloang Pass, west Pohnpei

Depth Range: 20-130ft+ (6-40m+)

Access: Boat

Expertise Rating: Intermediate

swim slowly and exhale gently. On afternoon dives, observe the big bulbs of closed magnificent anemones with their hovering clownfish. The nasty coral bleaching that hit most of the Pacific did not affect Pohnpei, so the anemones still have their natural and diverse coloration. Lionfish, soft corals, flatworms and nudibranchs, crinoids, brilliant purple lace corals and a host of other critters make this a great macro dive.

Colonial anemones and crinoids become underwater art.

42 Poahloang Mouth

As you approach the mouth of the pass, the palm-studded islands of Ahnd Atoll are visible in the distance. At high tide,

Location: Poahloang Pass, west Pohnpei

Depth Range: 30-130ft (10-40m)

Access: Boat

Expertise Rating: Advanced

the water clarity is incredible and a moderate kick through the upper reef current puts you on an active and exciting sloping wall. This dive can also be combined with a drift down the Poahloang Pass, but is a fine deep dive by itself, promising big critters like grey reef sharks, silvertip sharks, silver mackerel, Napoleon wrasse and jacks cruising singly and in pairs.

The healthy corals attract multicolored lionfish whose sharp and poisonous dorsal fins you should try to avoid. Soft corals and spindly crinoids add rich color and diversity. Spinner dolphins also visit the outer reef waters. Watch the surface action as birds swoop in while large schools of yellowfin tuna feed.

Lionfish hide in the coral crevices.

A diver marvels at the sea star and lush soft corals.

43 Dawahk Pass

This channel-mouth dive, which can lead to a drift into the channel or a drift to the outer reef wall, promises excitement from the very start. Dive at high, incoming tide for the best visibility and observe the amazing lineup of large Napoleon wrasse at the reeftop. Fusiliers run along the ridge in bright shocks of electric blue. Look for one or more eagle rays swimming into the current. They come fairly close to divers, so close you

Location: Dawahk Pass, west Pohnpei

Depth Range: 30-130ft (10-40m)

Access: Boat

Expertise Rating: Advanced

can often see their barbed tailbase and the spots on their backs.

Look into the blue for grey reef sharks and the occasional dogtooth tuna. Many sizes and hues of sea fans grow at the deeper reaches. The outside wall produces a fine cast of fish and macro invertebrates. Coral hermit crabs, Christmas tree worms of all sizes, big-eyed spotted blennies, lionfish and stonefish join tridacna clams and feeding crinoids. This is a nice, leisurely swim that doesn't necessitate super deep diving.

SUSANNA HINDERKS

A sea star starts to regenerate a couple of lost arms.

44 Inner Sanctum

This great little coral dive was found when a biologist specializing in corals asked local diver Wendolin Lionis where to go to find good coral cover. After many experimental dives they found this site, chock-full of corals. Deep fingers and shallow slopes are filled with plate corals, groves of staghorns and some really oddball hard coral formations that have developed over decades of growth. The protected

Location: Inner Palikir lagoon

Depth Range: 2-100ft (1-30m)

Access: Boat

Expertise Rating: Novice

tranquil nature of this inner-lagoon site makes it a unique sanctum indeed.

This is also a good spot for macro-photography and for fish photographers, although visibility is not always great. The nutrients are good for the corals but not for divers wanting gin-clear water. Try diving at slack high tide and spend lots of time in the shallows observing the good invertebrate life.

Upper reef areas inside the lagoon support healthy coral growth.

45 Palikir Pass

This flirt with excitement is one of Pohnpei's—and Micronesia's—premier dives. It is a short boat ride from the Kolonia Harbor, and the promontory of Sokehs Rock sits boldly nearby. This dive is always an adrenalin rush, as the Palikir Pass is one of the most active in Pohnpei. The site's biggest claim to fame is the almost ever-present school of grey reef sharks.

The key is to dive on incoming tide or visibility will greatly diminish. A deep reef runs across the mouth of the channel.

Location: Palikir Pass mouth

Depth Range: 20-130ft+ (6-40m+)

Access: Boat

Expertise Rating: Intermediate

The dive is normally made starting out-side the channel mouth and proceeding down, across the mouth and along the deep reef. The school of grey reefs range in size from juveniles to full-grown adults and get together in groups of 30 to over 100, depending on the day and speed of the tide movement. Divers can nestle down and hug the reef at 120ft or so, and the sharks will come fairly close. This limits bottom time and increases air use, but the excitement is worth it as a seemingly endless parade of greys comes by, standing out against the blue backdrop.

Depending on the current direction, either continue the dive by swimming across the mouth to the other side and drift in, or swim back and drift in on the entry side. Large coral mounds with cuts and crevices mark the upper reef at the mouth. It then turns into a sloping wall—a fine place to find anemones, lace corals, small gorgonian sea fans and small soft corals.

The fish life is fantastic. Look for large schools of jacks, black bar barracuda, sweetlips and snapper. Healthy populations of Napoleon wrasse and bumphead parrotfish are found hanging off the reef. King mackerel, wahoo and tuna also run along the reef, and large groupers linger on the slope. This pass can be exciting and provides many hours of diving thrills.

Aerial view of Sokehs Rock, Pohnpei's boldest landmark.

Crinoids and soft corals harbor a variety of macro marine life.

46 Palikir Wall

The Palikir Wall is a great place to find macro subjects and to check out unusual marine life. Shell-viewing can be quite good with giant Triton's trumpets, augers, tridacnas, large trochus and many cowrie species in the area. Along the wall, look for eels and the occasional sleeping turtle.

Location: Inner Palikir Pass

Depth Range: 30-120ft (9-37m)

Access: Boat

Expertise Rating: Intermediate

Start your dive near the tall, white channel marker and drift in. A giant coral head marks the turn at the point in the channel. The current tends to run through the sandy patches here and sleeping whitetip sharks rest in the open spaces. This is a popular place for big triggerfish to nest, but avoid them as they get a little ornary when nesting. Beautiful soft corals in many hues flank the coral heads. Look for striped pipefish, blennies, and anemones with their clownfish in the shallow coral garden.

Clown triggerfish nest in the reef's upper reaches.

Ahnd & Pakein Atolls

In the early summer months the seas around Pohnpei turn flat and glassy. A boat glides over the calm sea as if skimming across clouds. Sea birds wing their way to the boat and keep pace, their reflection dancing along the surface.

On the horizon, a mirage seems to appear. The atolls of Ahnd and Pakein, to the south and west of Pohnpei respectively, are images of pure beauty floating on the open sea. All of the stories about the amazing sea life and pristine beaches don't prepare visitors for the first real glance, both above and below the surface. Few people live on Pakein and Ahnd is uninhabited; crabs and sea birds are the main residents on both of these gems.

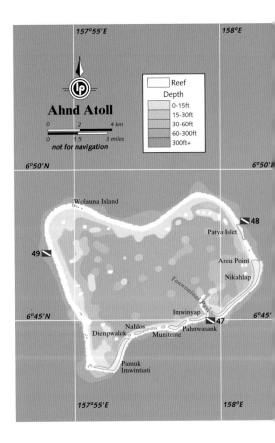

Ahnd's only channel offers a sheer drop-off—perfect for drift diving.

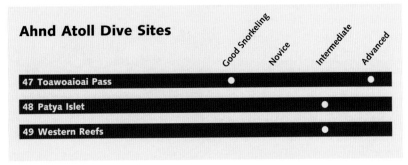

Ahnd Atoll Dive Sites

	Good Snorkeling	Novice	Intermediate	Advanced
47 Toawoaioai Pass	●			●
48 Patya Islet			●	
49 Western Reefs			●	

47 Toawoaioai Pass

Ahnd Atoll's beauty can bring tears to the eyes. The large Toawoaioai Pass opens to some of the most idyllic sand beaches in the Pacific. A snorkeler's paradise, the clear water along the drop-off displays coral beds and golden sea fans. Soft corals, fed by the massive influx and outflow of water, also adorn the walls. This is the atoll's only outlet for tidal flow, and it's quite narrow so currents really rip, making the sea life nothing short of eye-popping.

Experienced divers come here because the changing tides promise pelagic creatures such as sailfish, Pacific blue marlin, all sorts of rays, yellowfin tuna and the list goes on. Sharks include some extremely large oceanic whitetips as well as silvertips and greys. Listen for dolphins clicking underwater as well.

Both the pass walls can be good, but the west wall is the most colorful. It is called **Orange Wall** or **Golden Wall**. The east wall is **Nikahlap Areu Wall**. Many overhangs, caverns and grottoes are carved by the constant tidal action and sea whips, gorgonians and other invertebrates thrive here. In some places, light shafts lead straight through the reef. The lighting is best in the morning. Depending on the moon, a night drift dive can be a real rush on the ripping tides. Night drifts should only be attempted by experienced divers.

Inside the lagoon, the action doesn't stop. The water is deep and the coral formations are large and full of active marine life at a site called **Turtle Canyon**. It is actually an extension of the pass and got its name from a resident population of both

Location: Toawoaioai Pass

Depth Range: 10-130ft+ (6-40m+)

Access: Boat

Expertise Rating: Advanced

hawksbill and green sea turtles. They like to feed on the hydroids and rest in the canyon's corals.

This area also features another wonderful site, **Barracuda Cove**, on the northwest side of Toawoaioai Pass. Named after the schools of blackbar and longnose barracuda, both manta and eagle rays are also common. The depth here can run from 10 to 85ft.

A yellow crinoid bursts with color on the west wall.

48 Patya Islet

The outside dives at Ahnd Atoll can be as exciting as the inner lagoon forays. There are two good sites here: **Sweeper's Point,** named after local divemaster Wendolin "Sweeper" Lionas, and **Northeast Reef Corner.**

Location: Eastern reef face

Depth Range: 15-130ft+ (5-40m+)

Access: Boat

Expertise Rating: Intermediate

Visibility at both sites is usually excellent. This is another spot pelagic-lovers come to get a glimpse of incredible blue-water denizens. You can expect to see ocean-going sharks up to 15ft long. Big fish reports include Pacific blue marlin, dogtooth and yellowfin tuna. More common are eagle rays, big mackerel, blackbar and other schools of barracuda.

Nice coral cover includes large areas of plating corals. Mushroom and staghorn corals and a good community of hard corals occur at shallower depths, while the deeper regions feature gorgonian sea fans and lots of colorful soft corals.

Huge coral formations dominate at Sweeper's Point.

49 Western Reefs

This area offers incredible visibility, although swells and wave action sometimes prevent diving here; when it is calm, it can be superb. Over time, waves have carved caves, tunnels and blue holes all along this reef stretch, which starts in the middle of the western reef and runs to the northwest tip.

Location: Western reef face

Depth Range: 30-130ft+ (9-40m+)

Access: Boat

Expertise Rating: Intermediate

The interesting features begin at about 60ft and extend down into a blue abyss along sheer walls and steep slopes. **Black Iris Wall** is named for a deep, dark cave along the central part of the reef. **Blue Grottoes** is farther north and has scenic grottoes, tunnels and blue holes.

Bird Island Wall is also a maze of huge cuts, canyons and sea-fan-covered inner walls at the tip of the barrier reef.

Keep an eye out for pelagic action and look in the tunnels and caves for resting sharks. Encounters startling both shark and diver have had some heart pounding, but, to date, harmless results. Anemone life here is plentiful and there are some very interesting coral formations.

Great walls and undercuts hold gardens of gorgonian sea fans.

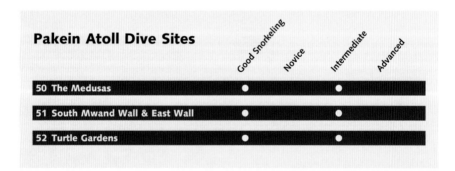

Pakein Atoll Dive Sites	Good Snorkeling	Novice	Intermediate	Advanced
50 The Medusas	●		●	
51 South Mwand Wall & East Wall	●		●	
52 Turtle Gardens	●		●	

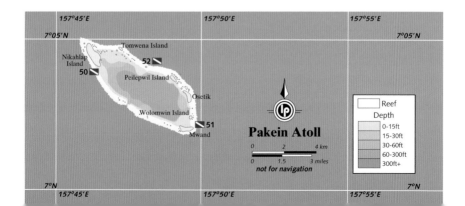

50 The Medusas

At the island's tip, the sea has gnawed into the outer reef wall, creating a massive overhang. Beneath this cliff a seemingly never-ending stream of crevalle jacks spews forth. Fast, silvery and sleek, they envelop you like an undulating blanket.

Location: Northwest Pakein

Depth Range: 10-130ft (3-40m)

Access: Boat

Expertise Rating: Intermediate

The dives in this area are considered Pakein's premier dives and offer superb water clarity, healthy corals and surprising fish action. Currents are strong at the points, but the inner coves can be quite mellow.

The Medusas, to the south of Nikahlap Island, is an amazing site. Deceptively deep, the clear water allows you a look at one of the most awe-inspiring grand canyons in the sea. Huge coral heads rise from the seafloor. Small sharks weave in and out of the passages. Brilliant crinoids sit atop rocky outcrops and bright, golden formations of lettuce coral spread across an area the size of a football field. Below, circling schools of barracuda rise to greet divers. There are five big Medusa-like coral heads and plenty of canyons, crevasses and coves along the wall heading east from the point. If dived on a calm day, this is a site most divers will remember for a long time.

On the north side of Nikahlap is **Reef Shark Bay** and, as the name implies, there are plenty of whitetip, silvertip and blacktip reef sharks along the reef and out on the sandy bottom.

The giant Medusas loom in Pakein's deep channels.

51 South Mwand Wall & East Wall

So, you want giant bumphead wrasses, eagle rays, sweetlips and wahoo? You came to the right place! South Mwand Wall has a varied topography with healthy and diverse wall and coral terraces that make excellent fish habitats. Although you can go deeper, most action takes place in the 40 to 90ft range.

At the southeast corner of the island a series of caves in the shallow range hold a plethora of marine invertebrate life, and close-up photography is quite good here.

At East Wall, a deep terrace features frequent visits by groups of eagle rays. But the finest feature here is the amaz-

Location: East and southeast Pakein

Depth Range: 5-130ft (2-40m)

Access: Boat

Expertise Rating: Intermediate

ing coral garden formations that start at about 65ft and run up the reef all the way to the surface. Exploration of these coral castles and bommies is well worth an entire dive.

Large lettuce coral formations are found all along the wall.

52   Turtle Gardens

The terrain here is markedly different than other Pakein topography and provides a good chance to see green sea turtles at the lower stretches of the reef.

Location: North central outer reef

Depth Range: 10-130ft (3-40m)

Access: Boat

Expertise Rating: Intermediate

Along the reef, nice stands of lettuce corals give amazing color to the site, highlighting the beautiful blue created by the reflective bottom. Staghorn corals are also abundant and, as a result, a good population of juvenile fish lingers in their thick protective branches.

Like anywhere you dive or snorkel in Pakein, this site combines great visibility, throbbing coral communities and a broad selection of marine life.

Feeding sea turtles give Turtle Gardens its name.

Feeding crinoids host a medley of small invertebrates.

In Kosrae, many people lead a traditional, natural lifestyle. It is not unusual to see men in dugout canoes paddling out to fish. Women use woven baskets to carry fruits to market. Riding a bamboo raft through the inlet with the incoming tide is a great source of fun and thrills for adventurous children.

For divers, there is still a lot to be discovered in Kosrae. Although many places in the world claim this, here it is true. Regular jet service started here in the late 1980s and early '90s, so diving tourism is still fairly new and small scale. The lack of development on Kosrae (the main road doesn't even go all the way around the island) keeps the reefs in superb shape. They are the kind you expect to see at an outer atoll. Fish life is plentiful.

Kosrae has the finest mooring buoy program in Micronesia. The sites around the entire island have well-maintained buoys and lines. Kosrae offers fine dive facilities, equipment, training and dedicated dive resorts.

Kosrae is a religious island and all businesses close on Sundays—by law. Diving is not permitted but it is OK to snorkel. Sundays are good days to hike into the pristine jungle or just read a book by the sea.

Kosrae Dive Sites

	Good Snorkeling	Novice	Intermediate	Advanced
53 Harbor Wrecks (Buoys 1 & 2)	●		●	
54 Village Reef (Buoy 4)	●	●		
55 Malem Reefs (Buoys 7 – 14)	●		●	
56 Hiroshi Point (Buoy 15)	●		●	
57 Utwe Coast (Buoys 16 & 17)	●		●	
58 Bully Hayes Wreck (Buoy 19)	●	●		
59 Walung Coral Gardens (Buoys 25 – 27)	●	●		
60 Walung Drop-Off (Buoys 29 & 30)	●		●	
61 Yela Wall (Buoys 36 & 37)			●	
62 Yela Channel (Buoys 37 & 38)	●		●	
63 Shark Island (Buoys 39 – 41)	●		●	
64 Blue Hole	●	●		

The sandy beaches near Malem are unmanicured and rife with natural beauty.

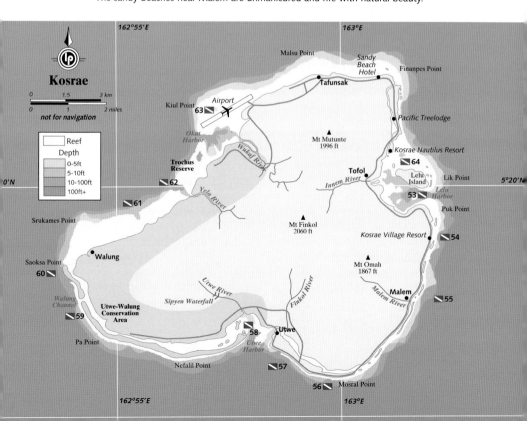

53 Harbor Wrecks (Buoys 1 & 2)

The dives in Lelu Harbor aren't known for their crystal-clear visibility. For divers comfortable with low visibility and a harbor environment, these dives are fun and a step back into history. One war victim is an amphibious bomber airplane. Located close to the harbor mouth, this plane is still mostly intact—take care when exploring to help keep it that way. This wreck has little coral growth but is an exciting find for wreck enthusiasts.

Farther in, a small Japanese freighter sits upright and is also intact, supporting coral growth and some invertebrate life.

Location: Lelu Harbor

Depth Range: 30-70ft (9-21m)

Access: Boat

Expertise Rating: Intermediate

The corals include wire, tubastrea and platter corals, and there are some encrusting sponges and a lot of fish life. There is bomb damage aft, showing what probably sank this 65ft-long ship. Visibility improves upon descent, but 30ft is still the average.

A resident barracuda school, batfish schools and lionfish like to feast on the baitfish around this wreck. Reports of extremely large grouper living in the holds are supposedly not exaggerated!

The remains of a 19th-century wooden whaler with some of its ribs still intact rest in the harbor, which has yet to be fully mapped and explored. Estimates suggest that three other planes (probably more) rest in the dark waters.

Tube corals growing on the wrecks.

54 Village Reef (Buoy 4)

The reef in front of the Kosrae Village Resort is a great place to observe sea life and see some unusual coral formations on a healthy and vibrant reef. You'll find large, branching staghorns and ample fairy basslets at 40 to 50ft. This is an abundantly fishy place with various groupers (including uncommon peacock groupers), scrawled filefish and beautiful regal angelfish.

The reef slope is not as dramatic as in some other places around Kosrae. Diving

Location: In front of Kosrae Village Resort

Depth Range: 25-80ft (8-24m)

Access: Boat

Expertise Rating: Novice

here is easy and sometimes done from buoy 4 over to buoy 5.

When it is calm, resort guests can also venture out over the reef to snorkel. The inner reef has a small tidal pool that is fun to walk around at low tide and deep enough to snorkel at high tide. Look for juvenile eels peeking out of crevices and marvel at the variety of sea birds living along this shoreline.

Huts at the Kosrae Village Resort are set in a natural mangrove forest.

Large clowfish flit about anemones and hard corals on the Village Reefs.

55 Malem Reefs (Buoys 7 – 14)

All along the Malem coast a series of buoys starts in fairly shallow water, getting somewhat deeper around buoys 13 and 14. When the swells are down and the sea is calm the whole coast is great to dive. On-land decompression stops between dives offer you a glimpse at the beautiful coastal mountains, with Mt. Omah's peak the most prominent.

Location: East coast

Depth Range: 25-90ft (8-27m)

Access: Boat

Expertise Rating: Intermediate

The changing underwater terrain keeps every dive fresh and exciting. Basslets flit about everywhere and table corals shelter a variety of fish and invertebrates. This area is a permanent coral-monitoring site—the condition of the coral is studied and documented regularly. Statistics from this work suggest that Kosrae's hard coral is among the healthiest and densest anywhere in Micronesia, or even anywhere in the world.

Beautiful table corals attest to the good health of reefs along the Malem coast.

56 Hiroshi Point (Buoy 15)

Hiroshi Point can be done as either a beach or boat dive, but the boat trip is recommended for getting right to the wall to start looking for action. The sloping drop-off at Hiroshi is covered in beautiful corals that are adorned by hovering fairy basslets in brilliant magentas and yellows.

Location: Southeast of Utwe Harbor

Depth Range: 20-110ft (6-34m)

Access: Boat/Beach

Expertise Rating: Intermediate

Take time to look around the current-swept overhangs for pastel soft-coral trees. Well-camouflaged stonefish and lizardfish like to wait for passing prey at these spots. Morays are also common in the many coral formations.

A good variety of sea anemones live here and schools of parrotfish roam the shallow waters, munching on corals and algae. Sand rays rest in the white sand flats around 20ft and big coral bommies come to within 15ft of the surface, making this an ideal snorkel site and a great place for novice divers to enjoy a truly beautiful reef. To top it off, you might see a pilot whale and get the rare opportunity to snorkel with it.

This is a favorite night diving spot right from the beach. Use the darkness as a chance to see shells and other small invertebrates that hide out during the day.

Sand rays bury themselves on the sandy bottom.

57 Utwe Coast (Buoys 16 & 17)

Snorkelers and divers alike will love this spot as it boasts healthy hard-coral cover. The coral ledges are a macro-photographer's dream, with a variety of nudibranchs, an artist's palette of Christmas tree worms and tiny shrimp. Eagle rays often lounge in the sandy patches.

Location: South of Utwe Harbor

Depth Range: 20-100ft (6-31m)

Access: Boat

Expertise Rating: Intermediate

Look for butterflyfish hiding in the many coral crevices. Brain corals grow quite large in this area. You can poke around for a long time, as a good variety of marine life hangs out in the 20 to 50ft range. Nice cabbage corals grow a little deeper. Approach slowly as fish sometimes like to rest in the recessed bases of these big, golden corals.

This is another fine night diving venue. Like Hiroshi Point, the invertebrate life—especially cowries—can really get active at night.

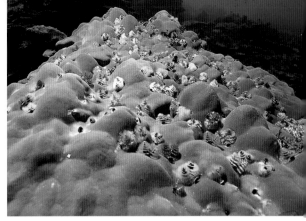

Utwe's hard corals host a forest of Christmas tree worms.

58 Bully Hayes Wreck (Buoy 19)

This may not be the world's best dive, but it is certainly a classic log entry. How many people can say they've dived a sunken pirate ship? The *Lenora*, the ship of scoundrel Bully Hayes, still has some visible wood and metal, although it is mostly silt-covered from run-off of a nearby river. The ship sank in 1874.

Bully Hayes was definitely not someone you'd want to bring home to Mother. He plundered virtually everything he saw on land and sea in the somewhat lawless days when whaling was big in Kosrae. By all reports he was hated by his crew, the locals and by his multiple wives. He finally met his demise when his ship's cook, who apparently didn't have the patience to poison Hayes, used a faster method and stabbed him with a knife.

Location: Utwe Harbor

Depth: 35ft (11m)

Access: Boat

Expertise Rating: Novice

This dive is sometimes done as a quick third dive if you have a little air left in your tank, but can be an interesting stand-alone dive, especially for muck divers. The wreck sits on a sandy bottom in a natural, deep harbor across from the Utwe Harbor dock. Look for juvenile lionfish and even small, sleeping turtles. Just west of the wreck is a good snorkeling spot for seeing small reef fish.

59 Walung Coral Gardens (Buoys 25 – 27)

This site's amazing coral display offers some absolutely huge and varied coral heads and big bunches of colorful Christmas tree worms. Morays hide within the cracks and crevices created by the thick, competitive corals.

Fantastic regal angelfish, absolutely brilliant flame angelfish, blackback but-

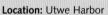

Location: Walung Channel

Depth Range: 35-80ft (11-24m)

Access: Boat

Expertise Rating: Novice

terflyfish, ornate butterfly-fish, midnight snapper and a whole collection of other reef fish make this a superb spot for fish-watchers. Look for shrimp and octopuses if the fish life gets too much to handle. All of this is found in the 40 to 60ft range. Deeper dives also produce sightings of sharks and pelagics. Current is usually minimal in here, making it a fine snorkeling site as well.

A reclusive moray escapes in a hard coral crevice.

Thick schools of anthias make Kosrae's drop-offs flash with color.

60 Walung Drop-Off (Buoys 29 & 30)

The untouched beaches and wild coast-line you'll see on the ride to this site are almost as great as the diving. The man-grove trees of the Trochus Reserve and neighboring Utwe-Walung Marine Park and mangrove conservation area tower against the lush green mountain peaks. Underwater, the greatness continues as reef sharks course a steep drop-off that is flushed by current and punctuated by large, healthy corals.

Location: Saoksa Point

Depth Range: 20-130ft (6-40m)

Access: Boat

Expertise Rating: Intermediate

Look for schooling barracuda and other large pelagics. Sea turtles are com-mon as are wrasses of all stages, with large Napoleons looming at the reeftop.

The reef is full of cleaning stations. Great barracuda and the Napoleons often stop here for a refresher. Spiny pufferfish are seen frequently, especially under overhangs where they sleep and rest. Anemones host huge orange-fin clownfish that Kosrae seems to special-ize in. Mat and carpet anemones are everywhere. Check out the broad array of tree worms. The whole reef is just an awesome display of healthy hard-coral cover.

A photographer takes advantage of a hardy stand of lettuce coral for a great photo subject.

61 Yela Wall (Buoys 36 & 37)

Location: South of Trochus Reserve

Depth Range: 40-120ft (12-37ft)

Access: Boat

Expertise Rating: Intermediate

The dive is somewhat deeper than most of the typical dives in Kosrae, starting at about 40ft atop a sloping wall and stretching to the blue abyss. The healthy hard corals host a broad collection of fish and invertebrates. It is possible to see large groups of scrawled filefish, which like to forage for food and get cleaned at the upper stations.

This area is fed by a lot of nutrients, as it is near the cut and an outlet to another mangrove conservation area. Look for eagle rays and scour the reef-top for macro subjects. Small mat sea anemones living among the reeftop castle corals host pairs of emperor shrimps.

62 Yela Channel (Buoys 37 & 38)

Location: South of Trochus Reserve

Depth Range: 25-90ft (8-27m)

Access: Boat

Expertise Rating: Intermediate

This sandy environment is a great place to watch the fish and invertebrates that prefer life away from the reef. A resident group of stingrays rests on the sandy bottom at around 90ft. Proximity to the conservation area makes this a great foraging site for rays, which comb the sand and mud in search of small invertebrates.

Look in the sand for garden eels that sway to and fro bobbing for food and planktonic particles. The stealthy eels disappear down into the sand when approached—as though they were never there—so be observant, move slowly and breathe lightly. Also look for pairings of gobies and bulldozer shrimp.

Sand creatures, such as spider conchs, thrive in the channel.

63 Shark Island (Buoys 39 – 41)

Shark Island is considered Kosrae's most accessible site for action, including a nice array of pelagic life such as grey reef and whitetip sharks, schooling barracuda and even large groups of dogtooth tuna. The currents here necessitate drift diving, making it a better site for more experienced divers.

Location: Western side, near airport

Depth Range: 20-130ft (6-40m)

Access: Boat

Expertise Rating: Intermediate

A favorite spot along the wall starts at about 40ft and drops to 70ft. Schooling eagle rays sometimes appear here. Look for them swimming in a "V"

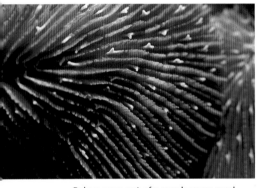

Polyps peep out of a purple razor coral.

formation like geese heading south for the winter.

Also look for rainbow runners speeding by in groups and for big schools of surgeonfish. When the current is running, photography can be challenging as the big fish tend to show up deeper on the reef. The experience is definitely worth the effort of bringing your camera along.

The upper reef features basslet schools, hard corals, sea turtles and colorful crinoids. During certain times of the year, literally dozens of stingrays have been observed here and are believed to be mating.

Strong currents fill the water with food for this grey reef shark.

A snorkeler scopes the reef, while the Sleeping Lady watches in the background.

64 Blue Hole

Diving or snorkeling the Blue Hole is a fun little venture and a unique log entry. This natural hole in the large inner-reef flat just in front of Kosrae Nautilus Resort is a breeding ground for juvenile fish.

The beach provides a pleasant, sandy walk. Access to the hole is easiest at high tide, as some coral patches and rocks need to be negotiated. The path of least resistance seems to be at the hole's north end. Kayaking the holes is a fun way to see them; either bring your snorkel or tow your BC and tank. The edge of the hole comes close to the surface in most places, so mooring a kayak is easy.

The hole's edges drop off vertically in some spots, and are lined with corals and other sessile marine growth. Schools of tiny baitfish, juvenile barracuda, angelfish and chromis hang out, along with nudibranchs. Rumor has it that a huge resident Pacific ray and some smaller

Location: Inner reef flat between main island and Lelu

Depth Range: 0-70ft (0-21m)

Access: Beach

Expertise Rating: Novice

ones live deep in the hole. Keep your eyes open for sea turtles and sharks—especially small foraging blacktips. As the sea constantly changes, so do the residents. Creatures have a habit of wandering into the reef flat and then get pulled back out when the tide changes. This makes diving here a constant surprise. If you're truly adventurous, look for the caverns created by freshwater upwellings.

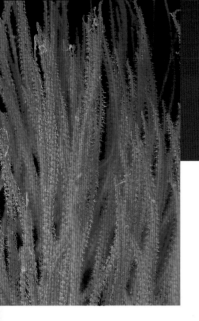

Marine Life

The marine life found in the Chuuk Lagoon and around Pohnpei and Kosrae is some of the most diverse in the Western Pacific. Chuuk's deep shipwrecks host excellent coral communities for a wide-variety of fish and invertebrates. Look in the sand, on crinoids and corals for interesting and unusual invertebrates. In the current-fed passes pelagics swoop in to feed in the waters that are fed by the ebb and flow of tidal currents. The listing below represents just a sampling of the great range of life found in this region.

Remember that common names are used freely but are notoriously inaccurate and inconsistent. The two-part scientific name, usually shown in italics, is more precise. It consists of a genus name followed by a species name. A genus is a group of closely related species that share common features. A species is a recognizable group within a genus whose members are capable of interbreeding. Where the species or genus is unknown, the naming reverts to the next known level: family (F), class (C) or phylum (Ph).

Common Vertebrates

manta ray
Manta birostris

purple anthias
Psuedanthias tuka

redfin anthias
Pseudanthias dispar

yellow coral goby
Gobiodon okinawae

neon damselfish
Pomacentrus coelestis

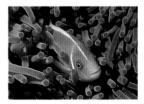

pink anemonefish
Amphiprion perideraion

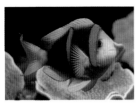

two-stripe anemonefish
F *Pomacentridae*

orange-fin anemonefish
Amphiprion chrysopterus

flame angelfish
Centropyge loriculus

regal angelfish
Pygoplites diacanthus

longnose butterflyfish
Forcipiger flavissimus

bumphead parrotfish
Bolbometopon muricatum

bluntnose parrotfish
F *Scaridae*

bignose unicornfish
Naso Vlamingii

varigated lizardfish
Synodus variegatus

longnose hawkfish
Oxycirrhites typus

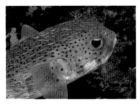

black-spotted porcupinefish
Diodon hystrix

scrawled filefish
Alutera scriptus

scrawled wrasse
F *Labridae*

trumpetfish
Aulostomus chinensis

reeftop pipefish
F *Syngnathidae*

Common Invertebrates

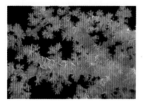

soft tree coral
F *Dendrophylliidae*

tubastrea coral
Tubastrea sp.

leather coral
Sarcophyton sp.

razor coral
Fungia sp.

cabbage coral
Turbinaria sp.

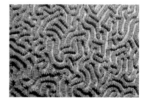

brain coral
Platygyra sp.

bubble coral
Plerogyra sp.

crinoid
Comanthina sp.

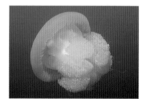

medusa jellyfish
Timoides agassizi

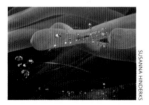

anemone shrimp
Periclimenes sp.

colonial anemone
Nemanthus sp.

tridacna clam
Tridacna squamosa

reticulated nudibranch
Reticulidia sp.

Christmas tree worm
Spirobranchus sp.

pillow sea star
Choriaster granulatus

Marine animals almost never attack divers, but many have defensive and offensive weaponry that can be triggered if they feel threatened or annoyed. The ability to recognize hazardous creatures is a valuable asset in avoiding accident and injury. The reefs in Micronesia are very diver-friendly. Respect the fish and marine creatures listed below and your diving experience will likely be incident free.

Fire Coral

Although often mistaken for stony coral, fire coral is a hydroid colony that secretes a hard, calcareous skeleton. It occurs throughout Micronesia, especially in channels. It is identifiable by its tan, mustard or brown color and finger-like columns with whitish tips. The colony is covered by tiny pores and fine, hair-like projections. Fire coral "stings" by discharging small, specialized cells called nematocysts. Contact causes a burning sensation that lasts for several minutes and

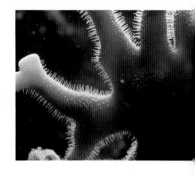

may produce red welts on the skin. Do not rub the area, as you will only spread the stinging particles. Cortisone cream can reduce the inflammation and antihistamine cream helps kill the pain. Serious stings should be treated by a doctor.

mastigias jellyfish

Jellyfish

These waters have no truly toxic jellyfish but there are many small jellyfish, such as the common mastigias, whose sting is irritating but not painful. Jellyfish sting by releasing the stinging cells contained in their trailing tentacles. As a rule, the longer the tentacles, the more painful the sting. Stings should be treated immediately with a decontaminant such as vinegar, rubbing alcohol, baking soda, papain, or dilute household ammonia. Beware that some people may have a stronger reaction than others, in which case you should prepare to resuscitate and seek medical aid.

Cone Shell

Viewing and photographing shells in the islands is a favorite pastime for many divers, but these beauties can be highly toxic. Do not touch or pick up cone shells. These mollusks deliver a venomous sting by shooting a tiny poisonous dart from their funnel-like pro-

BOB HALSTEAD

boscis. Stings will cause numbness and can be followed by muscular paralysis or even respiratory paralysis and heart failure. Immobilize the victim, apply a pressure bandage, be prepared to use CPR, and seek urgent medical aid.

Crown-of-Thorns Sea Star

This large sea star can have up to 23 arms, although 13 to 18 are more commonly observed. Body coloration can be blue, green or grayish with the spines tinted red or orange. The spines are venomous and can deliver a painful sting even if the animal has been dead for two or three days. Also beware the toxic pedicellariae (pincers) between the spines, which can also cause severe pain upon contact. To treat stings, remove any loose spines, soak stung area in nonscalding hot water for 30 to 90 minutes and seek medical aid. Neglected wounds may produce serious injuries. If you've been stung before, your reaction to another sting may be worse than the first.

LEN ZELL

Lionfish

Also known as turkeyfish or firefish, these slow, graceful fish extend their feathery pectoral fins as they swim. They have distinctive vertical brown or black bands alternating with narrower pink or white bands. When threatened or provoked, lionfish may inject venom through dorsal spines that can penetrate booties, wetsuits and leather gloves. The wounds can be extremely painful. If stung, wash the wound and immerse in nonscalding hot water for 30 to 90 minutes. Administer pain medications if necessary.

Scorpionfish

These well-camouflaged creatures have poisonous spines along their dorsal fins. They are often difficult to spot since they typically rest quietly on the bottom or on coral, looking more like rocks. Practice good buoyancy control and watch where you put your hands. Scorpionfish wounds can be excruciating. To treat a puncture, wash the wound and immerse in nonscalding hot water for 30 to 90 minutes. Administer pain medications if necessary.

Triggerfish

When you see the variety and size of trigger-fish in these islands, their placement under "hazardous" here doesn't seem so amusing. Bites from the larger moustache triggerfish can draw blood. If a fish chases you, stay away from its nesting area and move on quickly. Treat bites with antiseptics, anti-tetanus and antibiotics.

Moray Eel

Distinguished by their long, thick, snake-like bodies and tapered heads, moray eels come in a variety of colors and patterns. Don't feed them or put your hand in a dark hole—eels have the unfortunate combination of sharp teeth and poor eyesight and will bite if they feel threatened. If you are bitten, don't try to pull your hand away suddenly—the teeth slant backward and are extraordinarily sharp. Let the eel release it and then surface slowly. Treat with antiseptics, anti-tetanus and antibiotics.

LEN ZELL

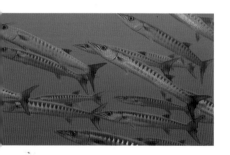

Barracuda

Barracuda are identifiable by their long, silver, cylindrical bodies and razor-like teeth protruding from an underslung jaw. They swim alone or in small groups, continually opening and closing their mouths, an action that looks daunting, but actually assists their respiration. Though barracuda will hover near divers to observe, they are really somewhat shy, though they may be attracted by shiny objects that resemble fishing lures. Irrigate bites with fresh water and treat with antiseptics, anti-tetanus and antibiotics.

Shark

Sharks are found on the wrecks, near current lines and along walls and passes. Most common are grey reef sharks and whitetips, both of which are not normally aggressive toward divers. Virtually all shark attacks in the islands have taken place in conjunction with spearfishing. Avoid spearfishing, carrying fish baits or mimicking a wounded fish and your likelihood of being attacked will greatly diminish. Face and quietly watch any shark that is acting aggressively and be prepared to push it away with camera, knife or tank. If someone is bitten by a shark, stop the bleeding, reassure the patient, treat for shock and seek immediate medical aid.

Diving Conservation & Awareness

All of the wrecks in Chuuk Lagoon are protected as historical monuments; disturbing or removing any artifact is illegal. Video or still photography is the best way to record a visit to these beautiful ships and islands. The Weno-based Society for Historic Investigation and Preservation (SHIP) works to educate locals and visiting divers on ways to protect the wrecks and their underwater environment.

On Pohnpei, a number of cultural restrictions keep both reef and land areas protected. Visitors cannot take away anything from the reef or land, be it a shell or a stone. Recent initiatives by Micronesian Islands Conservation, Inc., a small group working to protect Pohnpei's resources, include the establishment of a marine sanctuary and marine monitoring program.

Kosrae's Utwe-Walung Marine Park includes the Trochus Reserve and Walung Conservation Area. The marine park's founder, Madison Nena, is an Indigenous Conservationist award-winner for his work educating the local community. Mangrove tours of the conservation areas provide a glimpse of the low-growing marine trees and the natural mazes they create. All mooring buoys in Kosrae are also protected and cannot be tampered with.

On all of the islands, photography is encouraged as a positive way to "take" souvenirs. Collecting any marine creatures—even fishing around the reefs—is frowned upon. The FSM has some wonderful natural resources above and below the sea and visitors are expected to help maintain the integrity of these wonderful yet fragile ecosystems.

Responsible Diving

Dive sites tend to be located where the reefs and walls display the most beautiful corals and sponges. It only takes a moment—an inadvertently placed hand or knee, or a careless brush or kick with a fin—to destroy this fragile, living part of our delicate ecosystem. By following certain basic guidelines while diving, you can help preserve the ecology and beauty of the reefs:

1. Never drop boat anchors onto a coral reef and take care not to ground boats on coral. Encourage dive operators and regulatory bodies in their efforts to establish permanent moorings at appropriate dive sites.

2. Practice and maintain proper buoyancy control and avoid over-weighting. Be aware that buoyancy can change over the period of an extended trip. Initially you may breathe harder and need more weighting; a few days later you may breathe

Preserving Shipwrecks

While many factors cause a wreck to deteriorate—the circumstances of its sinking, weather conditions, water temperature, wave and current action—divers can do a few things to slow the disintegration process:

Be Aware After a ship sinks and the paint decays, marine animals settle in and their presence delays corrosion and decay. Protecting marine life is an important part of wreck preservation. Be especially careful with your fins, bubbles, hands´ and tank to prevent breaking coral and marine growth.

Cautious Anchoring Imprudent anchoring also damages sessile growth and speeds corrosion where an anchor is repeatedly placed. Moor on buoys where possible or anchor in sand.

Reduce Wake In areas where shallow shipwrecks are known to rest, boats should slow down in order to reduce wake.

No Take Help maintain historical significance and structural integrity of ships by following a strict "look but don't touch" approach.

Shipwrecks are like pieces of art in a museum; they should be admired but not touched.

more easily and need less weight. Tip: Use your weight belt and tank position to maintain a horizontal position—raise them to elevate your feet, lower them to elevate your upper body. Also be careful about buoyancy loss: as you go deeper, your wetsuit compresses, as does the air in your BC.

3. Avoid touching living marine organisms with your body and equipment. Polyps can be damaged by even the gentlest contact. Never stand on or touch living coral. The use of gloves is no longer recommended: gloves make it too easy to hold on to the reef. The abrasion caused by gloves may be even more damaging to the reef than your hands are. If you must hold on to the reef, touch only exposed rock or dead coral.

4. Take great care in underwater caves. Spend as little time within them as possible, as your air bubbles can damage fragile organisms. Divers should take turns inspecting the interiors of small caves or under ledges to lessen the chances of damaging contact.

5. Be conscious of your fins. Even without contact, the surge from heavy fin strokes near the reef can do damage. Avoid full-leg kicks when diving close to the bottom and when leaving a photo scene. When you inadvertently kick something, stop kicking! It seems obvious, but some divers either panic or are totally oblivious when they bump something. When treading water in shallow reef areas, take care not to kick up clouds of sand. Settling sand can smother the delicate reef organisms.

6. Secure gauges, computer consoles and the octopus regulator so they're not dangling—they are like miniature wrecking balls to a reef.

7. When swimming in strong currents, be extra careful about leg kicks and handholds.

8. Photographers should take extra precautions as cameras and equipment affect buoyancy. Changing f-stops, framing a subject and maintaining position for a photo often conspire to prohibit the ideal "no-touch" approach on a reef. When you must use "holdfasts," choose them intelligently (i.e., use one finger only for leverage off an area of dead coral).

9. Resist the temptation to collect or buy coral or shells. Aside from the ecological damage, taking home marine souvenirs depletes the beauty of a site and spoils other divers' enjoyment.

10. Ensure that you take home all your trash and any litter you may find as well. Plastics in particular pose a serious threat to marine life.

11. Resist the temptation to feed fish. You may disturb their normal eating habits, encourage aggressive behavior or feed them food that is detrimental to their health.

12. Minimize your disturbance of marine animals. Don't ride on the backs of turtles or manta rays as this can cause them great anxiety.

Marine Conservation Organizations

The following groups are actively involved in promoting responsible diving practices, publicizing environmental marine threats, and lobbying for better policies.

Micronesian Organizations

Micronesian Islands Conservation, Inc.
P.O. Box 159
Kolonia, Pohnpei 96941, FSM
☎ 691-320-2480
fax: 691-320-2479

Society for Historic Investigation & Preservation (SHIP)
P.O. Box 57
Weno, Chuuk 96942, FSM
☎ 691-330-4096
fax: 691-330-4096

Utwe-Walung Marine Park (Conservation Area)
P.O. Box 539
Utwe, Kosrae 96944, FSM
☎ 691-370-3483
fax: 691-370-5839
MarinePark@mail.fm

International Organizations

CORAL: The Coral Reef Alliance
☎ 510-848-0110
www.coral.org

Coral Forest
☎ 415-788-REEF
www.blacktop.com/coralforest

Cousteau Society
☎ 757-523-9335
www.cousteausociety.org

Ocean Futures
☎ 805-899-8899
www.oceanfutures.com

Project AWARE Foundation
☎ 714-540-0251
www.projectaware.org

ReefKeeper International
☎ 305-358-4600
www.reefkeeper.org

Telephone Calls

To call Chuuk, Pohnpei or Kosrae, dial the international access code for the country you are calling from (from the U.S. it's 011) + 691 (the FSM's country code) + the 7-digit local number.

Diving Services

Chuuk

**Blue Lagoon Dive Shop
(Blue Lagoon Resort)**
P.O. Box 429
Weno, Chuuk 96942, FSM
BLDiveshop@mail.fm
☎ 330-2796 fax: 330-4307
www.truk-lagoon.com
Sales: yes **Rentals**: yes
Air: yes **Courses**: no
Boats: 9 x 28ft-fiberglass boats, with twin 40hp engines
Trips: Daily trips to wrecks, reefs and Jeep Island

Chuuk Pacific Resort
P.O. Box 123
Weno, Chuuk 96942, FSM
☎ 330-2723 fax: 330-2729
GOCPR@mail.fm
www.gochuuk.com
Sales: no **Rentals**: yes
Air: yes **Courses**: no
Boats: 2 x 32ft with outboards
Trips: Daily trips to wrecks

Micronesia Aquatics of Truk Lagoon
P.O. Box 57
Weno, Chuuk 96942, FSM
☎ 330-4096 fax: 330-4096
cgraham@mail.fm
Sales: no **Rentals**: no
Air: no **Courses**: no
Boats: Fiberglass with outboard
Trips: Trips to wrecks and reefs; small groups by appointment only

Sundance Tours and Dive Shop
P.O. Box 85
Weno, Chuuk 96942, FSM
☎ 330-4234 fax: 330-4334
sundance@mail.fm
www.divetruklagoon.com
Sales: yes **Rentals**: yes
Air: yes **Courses**: no
Boats: Pro 42 jet-powered Rob Shirley dive boat; 1 x 34ft with outboard, 2 x 23ft with outboards
Trips: Daily trips to wrecks and reefs

Pohnpei

Aqua World Pohnpei, Inc.
(Pwohmaria Beach Resort)
P.O. Box 243
Kolonia, Pohnpei 96941, FSM
☎ 320-5941 fax: 320-2391
pwohmariabeach@mail.fm
Sales: no **Rentals**: yes
Air: yes **Courses**: Open Water
Boats: 2 x covered fiberglass skiffs
Trips: To all Pohnpei sites including
Ahnd and Pakein Atolls; night dives;
manta dives

Iet Ehu Tours
P.O. Box 559
Kolonia, Pohnpei 96941, FSM
☎ 320-2958 fax: 320-2958
Sales: no **Rentals**: limited
Air: yes **Courses**: Open Water &
Advanced
Boats: 2 x 28ft outboards with sun
cover
Trips: To all Pohnpei sites including
Ahnd and Pakein Atolls
Other: Kayak, cultural, camping and
hiking tours available

Phoenix Marine Sports Club
P.O. Box 387
Kolonia, Pohnpei 96941, FSM
☎ 320-2362/2363 fax: 320-2364
Sales: yes **Rentals**: yes
Air: yes **Courses**: no
Boats: 2 x 30ft; 1 x 40ft; 1 x 55ft, all
with twin engines
Trips: To all Pohnpei sites including
Ahnd and Pakein Atolls

Village Tour and Dive Service
(The Village Hotel)
P.O. Box 339
Pohnpei 96941, FSM
☎ 320-2797 fax: 320-3797
thevillage@mail.fm
Sales: no **Rentals**: limited
Air: yes **Courses**: no
Boats: 27ft covered skiff with twin
50hp outboard; 25ft covered skiff with
twin 55hp outboard; 23ft covered skiff
with outboard
Trips: To all Pohnpei sites including Nan
Madol and Ahnd Atoll; night dives
available
Other: Kayak tours available

Kosrae

Phoenix Marine Sports Club
P.O. Box PHM
Lelu, Kosrae 96944, FSM
☎ 370-3100 fax: 370-3509
Sales: yes **Rentals**: yes
Air: yes **Courses**: no
Boats: 2 x covered boats with twin
engines
Trips: Daytrips (except Sunday) to all
top Kosrae sites

Dive Caroline
(Sandy Beach Hotel)
P.O. Box 6
Tafunsak, Kosrae 96944, FSM
☎ 370-3239 fax: 370-2109
Sales: yes **Rentals**: yes
Air: yes **Courses**: no
Boats: Catamaran (8 divers); Bayliner
(10 divers)
Trips: Daytrips (except Sunday) to all
top Kosrae sites

Kosrae (continued)

**Sleeping Lady Divers
(Kosrae Village Resort)**
P.O. Box 399
Teyah, Kosrae 96944, FSM
☎ 370-3483 fax: 370-5839
kosraevillage@mail.fm
www.kosraevillage.com
Sales: yes **Rentals**: yes
Air: yes, nitrox available **Courses**: Open
Water to Advanced; 16 specialties
Boats: 2 x 26ft catamarans with full sun
canopies
Trips: Daytrips (except Sunday) to all
top Kosrae sites
Other: PADI 5-star dive center; IANTD
Tech diving center; rental kayaks available

Kosrae Nautilus Resort
P.O. Box 135
Kosrae 96944, FSM
☎ 370-3567 fax: 370-3568
nautilus@mail.fm
www.diveguideint.com/p0260.htm
Toll-free: 800-634-5555
Sales: yes **Rentals**: yes
Air: yes **Courses**: Open Water to
Divemaster; range of specialties
Boats: 28ft aluminum, with on-board
compressor, 250hp outboard; 23ft
fiberglass with twin 70hp outboard
Trips: Daytrips (except Sunday) to all
top Kosrae sites
Other: PADI 5-star dive center; sport
fishing tours available

Live-Aboards

Truk *Aggressor II*
P.O. Drawer K 5002, Hwy 90
East Morgan City, LA 70381, USA
☎ 504-385-2628 fax: 504-384-0817
103261.1275@compuserve.com
www.aggressor.com
Home Port: Blue Lagoon Resort
Boat Description: 107ft aluminum dive
yacht; boat moves around the lagoon
and divers dive from this boat or from
tenders on outer reef sites
Accommodations: 7 staterooms with
A/C, private baths
Passengers: 16-diver capacity
Destinations: 7-day trips in the lagoon
and to outer reefs, 5½ diving days daily
Season: January through July
Other: Nitrox and Nitrox Diver courses
available; PADI/NAUI certification and
specialty courses; underwater photography courses; camera and gear-rinse
facilities; video and photo labs with
daily E6 processing; underwater
ecology seminars; nightly slide show;
open-air hot tub on-deck fits 6 divers;
airport transfers

Truk *Odyssey*
4417 Beach Blvd. Suite 200
Jacksonville, FL 32207, USA
☎ 800-757-5396 fax: 904-346-0664
info@trukodyssey.com
www.TrukOdyssey.com
Home Port: Weno
Boat Description: 126ft converted
passenger cruise ship; boat moves
around the lagoon and divers dive right
from the boat
Accommodations: 9 staterooms (7 dbl,
2 single) with A/C, private baths
Passengers: 16-diver capacity
Destinations: 7-day trips in the lagoon
and to outer reefs, 5 dives daily
Season: Year-round
Other: Full technical diving services,
fixed deco bar, free nitrox; PADI certification courses include technical diving;
camera and gear-rinse facilities; on-
bard E6 processing, battery charger,
slide table, video viewing; darkroom
and viewing area; airport transfers

SS *Thorfinn*
P.O. Box DX
Weno, Chuuk 96942, FSM
☎ 330-4302 fax: 330-4253
Seaward@mail.fm
www.thorfinn.net
Home Port: Weno
Boat Description: 170ft converted classic whaler. Fiberglass and aluminum tenders take divers to dive sites.
Accommodations: 11 staterooms with A/C, private or semi-private baths.

Passengers: 22-diver capacity
Destinations: Weekly trips in the lagoon and outer reefs, 5 dives daily including night dives
Season: Year-round
Other: Emergency O2; camera and gear-rinse facilities; darkroom and viewing area; open-air hot tub on deck fits 12 divers; airport transfers

Tourist Offices

The local tourist offices are valuable resources when planning your trip. The FSM government operates a website (www.fsmgov.org) that provides information on FSM geography, history, politics and tourism. Once you arrive in Chuuk, Pohnpei and Kosrae, you'll find helpful staff and excellent local information at the islands' tourist offices.

Tourist Offices

Pohnpei Visitors Bureau
P.O. Box 1949
Kolonia, Pohnpei 96941, FSM
☎ 320-4851/4823 fax: 320-4868
pohnpeiVB@mail.fm

Chuuk Visitors Bureau
P.O. Box FQ
Weno, Chuuk 96942, FSM
☎ 330-4133 fax: 330-2233
cvb@mail.fm

Kosrae Office of Tourism
P.O. Box 1075
Kosrae, 96944, FSM
☎ 370-2228 fax: 370-2066
kosrae@mail.fm

Index

dive sites covered in this book appear in **bold** type

Lonely Planet Pisces Books

The **Diving & Snorkeling** guides cover top destinations worldwide. Beautifully illustrated with full-color photos throughout, the series explores the best diving and snorkeling areas and prepares divers for what to expect when they get there. Each site is described in detail, with information on suggested ability levels, depth, visibility and, of course, marine life. There's basic topside information as well for each destination.

Also check out dive guides to:

Lonely Planet Series Descriptions

Lonely Planet **travel guides** explore a destination in depth with options to suit a range of budgets. With reliable, practical advice on getting around, restaurants and accommodations, these easy-to-use guides also include detailed maps, color photographs, extensive background material and coverage of sites both on and off the beaten track.

For budget travelers **shoestring guides** are the best single source of travel information covering an entire continent or large region. Written by experienced travelers these 'tried and true' classics offer reliable, first-hand advice on transportation, restaurants and accommodations, and insider tips for avoiding bureaucratic confusion and stretching money as far as possible.

City guides cover many of the world's great cities with full-color photographs throughout, front and back cover gatefold maps, and information for every traveler's budget and style. With information for business travelers, all the best places to eat and shop and itinerary suggestions for long and short-term visitors, city guides are a complete package.

Lonely Planet **phrasebooks** have essential words and phrases to help travelers communicate with the locals. With color tabs for quick reference, an extensive vocabulary, use of local scripts and easy-to-follow pronunciation instructions, these handy, pocket-sized language guides cover most situations a traveler is likely to encounter.

Lonely Planet **walking guides** cover some of the world's most exciting trails. With detailed route descriptions including degrees of difficulty and best times to go, reliable maps and extensive background information, these guides are an invaluable resource for both independent hikers and those in organized groups.

Lonely Planet **travel atlases** are thoroughly researched and fact-checked by the guidebook authors to ensure they complement the books. The handy format means none of the holes, wrinkles, tears or constant folding and refolding of flat maps. They include background information in five languages.

Journeys is a new series of travel literature that captures the spirit of a place, illuminates a culture, recounts an adventure and introduces a fascinating way of life. Written by a diverse group of writers, they are tales to read while on the road or at home in your favorite armchair.

Entertaining, independent and adventurous, Lonely Planet **videos** encourage the same approach to travel as the guidebooks. Currently broadcast throughout the world, this award-winning series features all original footage and music.

Lonely Planet Online

Get the latest travel information before you leave or while you're on the road

Whether you've just begun planning your next trip, or you're chasing down specific info on currency regulations or visa requirements, check out Lonely Planet Online for up-to-the-minute travel information.

As well as travel profiles of your favorite destinations (including maps and photos), you'll find current reports from our researchers and other travelers, updates on health and visas, travel advisories, and discussion of the ecological and political issues you need to be aware of as you travel.

There's also an online travelers' forum where you can share your experience of life on the road, meet travel companions and ask other travelers for their recommendations and advice. We also have plenty of links to other online sites useful to independent travelers.

And of course we have a complete and up-to-date list of all Lonely Planet travel products including guides, phrasebooks, atlases, Journeys and videos and a simple online ordering facility if you can't find the book you want elsewhere.

www.lonelyplanet.com or **AOL keyword: lp**

Lonely Planet Publications

Australia
P.O. Box 617, Hawthorn, Victoria 3122
☎ (03) 9819 1877 fax: (03) 9819 6459
email: talk2us@lonelyplanet.com.au

USA
150 Linden Street
Oakland, California 94607
☎ (510) 893 8555, (800) 275 8555
fax: (510) 893 8563
email: info@lonelyplanet.com

UK
10a Spring Place,
London NW5 3BH
☎ (0171) 428 4800 fax: (0171) 428 4828
email: go@lonelyplanet.co.uk

France
1 rue du Dahomey
75011 Paris
☎ 01 55 25 33 00 fax: 01 55 25 33 01
email: bip@lonelyplanet.fr

www.lonelyplanet.com